Praise for

PASSIONATE PRACTICE

"Delightful…Elson takes psychological concepts that are actually quite complicated…and simplifies them for us into an approach to learning music that ultimately frees us to bring our very selves (warts and all, as she says) into the music we play…she shows us how to flip the demon, anxiety, into a catalyst rather than impediment in playing."

 – *The California Music Teacher*, Fall, 2002

"The book delineates how we can…practice efficiently, overcome performance fears and find our expressive voice. The strongest contribution here is the variety of psychological devices; if one strategy doesn't connect with a reader, it's quite likely that another one will – and this is good, since the dynamics of performance psychology are so very personal."

 – *American Music Teacher*, February / March 2003

"The best book I've read in the field of music-making. Non-musicians as well as musicians will profit from it because the scope is so broad. One of the most genuinely meaningful books on performing I've ever read; the examples are truly striking and to the point."

 – Ken Bruckmeier, Professor Emeritus of Music

"…the author's techniques are easily extrapolated to [all] instruments and to singers, actors and dancers. Essentially, these are the skills needed to develop good practice and performance habits, regardless of the instrument or performance style."

 – *Medical Problems of Performing Artists*, Fall, 2003

"I have found this book not only profound but also comforting in its optimism. AND – it's a great distraction from awful thoughts at 4 AM – for that alone, I think it's terrific."

 – Sally Weare, MFA. Internationally exhibited artist, educator.

"*Passionate Practice* is full of creative, insightful, and practical ideas that will aid musicians in practicing, teaching and performing. Margret Elson has provided us with beautiful steps toward attaining mind/body wholeness. And it is beautifully written. I highly recommend it to students and colleagues."

– Phyllis Lehrer, Professor of Piano, Westminster Choir College of Rider University

"This book is especially for musicians who are having difficulty engaging their passions in the hard, methodical work that is needed to acquire and sustain mastery of an instrument or to memorize a body of repertoire. Her unorthodox graphic illustrations and verbal imagery will be liberating to many readers…her approach shows a profound empathy for the struggles of every…disaffected musician. This is a kind, generous and helpful book."

– *Music for the Love of It*, December, 2002

"*Passionate Practice* enabled me to develop a sense of peace that I could return to again and again in the midst of performance. It furthered a faith that with proper training, I could count on my thoughts and words to come even if I felt temporarily lost."

– Mitchell Newman, M.D., playwright, actor, director, teacher, Artistic Director, *Thirsty Theater Acting Lab*, New York City

"This book has wide application, especially because the ideas and training exercises are so specific and geared to helping people learn an extremely complex skill. Whether it be playing the piano in public or talking to a psychotherapy client about changing 'old scripts' in relationships, the principles are the same. One can re-model the exercises for the skill being learned. A rare contribution."

– Louise Bettner, PhD., Clinical Psychologist, Classical Pianist, Faculty, John F. Kennedy University

"*Passionate Practice* offers deep insights into our quest for self-mastery through music. It is a welcome and significant addition to our field."

– Seymour Bernstein

PASSIONATE PRACTICE
The Musician's Guide to Learning, Memorizing and Performing

PASSIONATE PRACTICE
The Musician's Guide to Learning, Memorizing and Performing

By

Margret Elson

REGENT PRESS

Oakland, CA

PASSIONATE PRACTICE: The Musician's Guide to Learning, Memorizing and Performing.
Copyright ©2002 by Margret Elson.

Library of Congress Cataloging-in-Publication Data

Elson, Margret.
    Passionate practice : the musician's guide to learning, memorizing, and performing / by Margret Elson.
    p. cm.
    Includes bibliographical references.
    ISBN 1-58790-021-1
    1. Instrumental music--Instruction and study. 2. Practicing (Music) I. Title

    MT170 .E47 2002
    781.4--dc21   2002023076

"The Avowal" by Denise Levertov, from *OBLIQUE PRAYERS*, copyright ©1984 by Denise Levertov, Reprinted by permission of New Directions Publishing Corp.

Cover Illustration and Interior Illustrations: Jack Myers, Design Site, Berkeley
Cover Design: Jack Myers, Design Site, Berkeley
Interior Design and Typesetting: Jack Myers, Tracy Dean, Tania Kac, Design Site, Berkeley
Printing and Binding: Allen Press, Kansas

Please address orders, inquiries, and correspondence to:
Regent Press
6020-A Adeline
Oakland, CA 94608
Phone: 510.547.7602
Fax: 510.547.6357
Email: regentpress@mindspring.com

Printed in the United States of America
10 9 8 7 6 5 4

Dedicated to my wonderful husband, Michael and surprisingly

sane sons, Lev and Ilan: together, the harmony of my life

In loving memory of my parents,

Ruth J. Elson

and

Jules J. Elson

Table of Contents

Acknowledgments

I feel deeply grateful for the emotional and practical support I received from my family and friends while writing and *angsting* over this book.

As always, the love and humor of my family is the fabric that sustains me through everything. Everlasting thanks to Michael, consistently there for me.

A very special thanks to a very special person, Linda Peterson, whose generosity of spirit, compassion and dedication to excellence are matched only by the many talents and extraordinary good-will she brings to all around her. I feel privileged to have her in my life and grateful for her on-going friendship and wisdom.

The deepest thanks to the friendships that carried me through the book process as lovingly as they carry me through the rest of my life: Marsha Sherman, Michael Cohen, Karen Carlson, Elizabeth Swarthout, Becca Jowitt, Susan Samson, Margie Samberg.

Many thanks both to the friends who read the manuscript with critical eye and colored pencil, and to the friends whose comments, supportive gestures and continual encouragement helped keep me going: Kathryn Fields, Linda Peterson, Karl Goldstein, John McCarthy, Laurette Goldberg, Maureen Draper, Louise Bettner, Jed Galant, Olya Katsman, Marta Winik, Diana Dabby, Susan Phillips, Jean Langmuir, Rachelle Goodfriend, Wendy Lichtman and her writers' group.

To my students and clients, who make me continually learn and refine, and who, by entrusting me with their most fearful demons, enable me to face my own: an enormous debt of gratitude.

Old debts of gratitude belong to Edgar Roberts, my piano teacher at Juilliard, Preparatory Division—special thanks for having given me an extraordinary musical foundation without the neurotic baggage that so often attends early music education. To Bonnie Epstein, psychotherapist—much appreciation for helping me reopen my life to beauty, creativity and passion. And to Dick Letts, who never shrank from a new idea and whose limitless imagination helped create fountains of artistic creativity.

INTRODUCTION

Divine Music is heard in every soul,
Continuous, resonant, self-sustaining

Guru Nanak
The First Sikh Guru

Of Music, Migraines and Metronomes

Let me tell you a story about how migraines changed my music-making.

It was twenty-five years ago at a routine eye appointment. When I told the doctor that I suffered from migraines all my life, he suggested I try biofeedback. I had no idea what that meant but anything that might alleviate migraines was worth a try.

During the next two months I went regularly to my biofeedback sessions. I was placed in a close, dark room where I lay hooked to a large machine with wires attached to forehead or fingertips. From the machine a loud clicking noise like an insistent metronome commanded attention. I was told to relax by imagining a warm, restful place like a beach. The object was to slow down the relentless clicking by becoming increasingly relaxed. With unseen sensitivity the metronome responded to the autonomic response it sensed from my skin. If it sensed tension, the clicking increased. If it sensed relaxation, it decreased.

Ever the good student, I immediately began to concentrate on getting the clicking to decrease. The more I tried, the faster the clicking. Finally, realizing I couldn't actively control the sound, I stopped trying. The sound decreased. Little by little, as I got out of my own way, my body found the right adjustments to rid itself of the metronomic clatter. When my mind wandered or became active, the clicking increased. When it let go into honest repose, the sound decreased.

Meanwhile back home, sitting up and practicing the piano, I noticed a remarkable change: I was much more focused than before, and I was learning new music more quickly.

What was going on?

I began to realize that I had been conditioned by the clicking sound to pay attention, in a state of passivity, to a stimulus. And that, while practicing, I would quickly and automatically refocus attention onto the music whenever my thoughts would stray.

A new revelation occurred while giving a recital. On the second line of the first page of the opening piece, I had a memory slip. Knowing I needed to repeat that page, my mind tightened as my fingers crept closer and closer to that spot. Giving myself one last mental directive, I took a deep breath and let my mind go on "inactive," (the same mode I assumed to decrease the biofeedback machine's clicking). Instinctively my body took over playing that passage which had been practiced umpteen million times. Immediately after playing the passage, I consciously brought my focus back to the music.

When I listened with great trepidation to the tape of that performance there was no audible glitch at that troublesome moment. I had discovered something momentous for myself: when my mind got out of the way, it was much easier to play.

As a teacher it became my goal to put all the components of what I had learned into a teachable method. While doing so the method began expanding to include information from psychology, behavioral science, body mechanics, neurobiology—anything in fact that would aid the student's quest for efficient learning, ease in playing, and predictability in performing. This book is that simple, step-by-step approach.

At the same time my career took a remarkable turn. Not only did my teaching become more subtle and dynamic but I also began counseling musicians facing musical and non-musical challenges impeding their musical growth. I had in fact created a new career I called Artistic Counseling. My clients and I worked on issues ranging from fear of performing concerts to fear of playing during lessons; from inability to concentrate to inability to change teachers when necessary; from fear of changing professions in order to become a musician to fear of changing professions in order to leave music. Suddenly I had dual careers—as teacher and as counselor—and was presenting my work at international conferences devoted to the integrated musician. Eventually I became a certified hypnotherapist and licensed psychotherapist.

Presently, one of the most fulfilling aspects of my career is working with fine musicians who also face emotional impediments outside the musical arena. I help them discover what I had discovered for myself: that making a breakthrough in one area of life leads to breakthroughs in other areas as well. And even though my students and I work primarily on their musical development, initial breakthroughs often occur in their personal and professional lives before occurring at the keyboard. Brenda, for example, mother of two pre-teens, began to experience better rapport with her children while she was learning better methods of focusing at the piano. Inadvertently she began taking more time and focusing more attention on them as we worked on taking more time and focusing attention on Mozart. "Mom, you don't seem as frazzled as you used to be," her daughter exclaimed. Likewise Robert, a lawyer who often was nervous when facing legal opponents, learned to breathe himself into a calm state and to engage with his opponents in a judicious frame of mind as we worked on his breathing at the keyboard.

Practice doesn't make perfect, it makes permanent.

Practice doesn't make perfect, it makes permanent, Master Teacher Alexander Libermann told his students, of whom I was privileged to be one. And practicing, like performing, is an art. I would like to invite you to discover in this book a method of artful practicing—both perfect and permanent—which ensures learning, memorizing and performing. With passion and confidence. And without migraines. Your route of discovery is a simple, incremental, step-by-step method of practicing. The premise of this integrative approach is that learning, memorizing and performing are not separate from each other; and that the performer can employ methods for succeeding in all those areas from the beginning.

You will find that the book often uses the keyboard in examples and exercises. That is because playing the piano was my second language, and I have been teaching and coaching pianists for over thirty years. However, each individual step in the method, as well as the overall method itself, is designed to enhance, and give security and confidence to any musician—to anyone, in fact, engaged in creative and artistic endeavors. Whatever your particular passion in life, you will find it simple to adjust any exercise to suit your own artistic needs. For the approach incorporates not only good musical techniques but sound psychological principles as well, based on my experience as psychotherapist, and as counselor to artists and performers for 25 years. Thus, passionate practice, based on the complementary views of teaching and psychology, is a powerful, integrated tool for optimum learning, memorizing and performing, whichever instrument you play, and in whatever area in life you aspire to attain security and confidence.

This book contains the means to free yourself from restricting modes of behavior and thought in order to feel the passionate exchange between you and your chosen endeavor.

As you traverse the road ahead, please bring along your sense of humor and willingness to be surprised. This, and lots of *patience, patience, patience.* That's as important as *practice, practice, practice.*

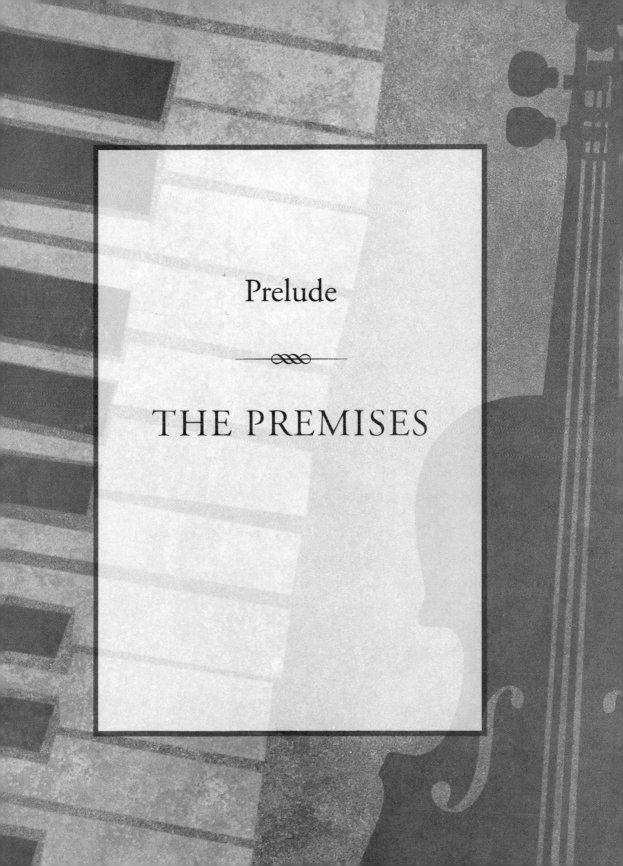

Prelude

⚬⚬⚬

THE PREMISES

The Premises

"Relax your shoulders."
"Let go of your tension."
"Look at the music."
"Don't look at the music."
"Look at the keyboard."
"Don't look at the keyboard."
"Listen to what I'm telling you."
"Listen to the music and you won't make mistakes."
"Think about the music and you won't be nervous."
"Don't think about anything. Just play."

Any of those sound familiar? Is there a music student alive whose teacher hasn't made those suggestions? The interesting thing is that most of those statements are true. Relaxing, focusing, looking, feeling, thinking, listening—all make better learning and playing. But *how* to relax, focus, listen, look, feel, and *how* to harness them to work together, automatically and simultaneously for both security and passion in performance—that is the challenge confronted in this book.

This book offers you a method to achieve your musical, your artistic goals based on exactly the premises about learning that underlay your teachers' suggestions. For beneath those ideas we find two basic premises about learning.

Those two basic premises about learning are:

- Learning is maximized when your mind is free to focus and your body free of unnecessary tension;
- Learning takes place through your senses, or sensory channels. In our work the most important sensory channels are:
    Auditory—hearing
    Visual—seeing
    Kinesthetic—feeling, movement, experience.

From those premises we conclude that you learn more quickly, efficiently and permanently when your mind is free, your body relaxed, your sensory channels open.

Learning means remembering. Most of us usually learn most quickly through personal experience: touching the hot stove, visiting foreign countries rather than reading about them. We experience those events most immediately through our senses: the pained and blistering finger (ouch); the sights, smells, sounds of Paris. But, *ahhh,* how we feel emotionally as a result of what happens to us is what seals the fate of our remembering: pain, fear of the stove; exhilaration, passion in Paris.

Another aspect of learning comes from focus and concentration. If you're engrossed in the last pages of a Stephen King thriller, you may miss the call to dinner. If your boyfriend proposes beneath the Eiffel Tower, you may miss its magnificence. But despite your attention being deflected from the grandeur of the monument at that fateful moment, you may be flooded with the feelings, sights and sounds of that night when you hear the word "Paris" years later. Intense emotion can embed an entire moment's gestalt in the recesses of your brain, even when you're not *consciously* aware of that taking place.

To sum up then, both focus and intensity of feeling are capable of producing "brain" memory, and it is possible to retain a deep memory of an event if we experienced a strong emotion at the time of its occurrence. Imagine, then, how memory can be enhanced if both focus and emotional intensity are consciously harnessed simultaneously. That is exactly what you will learn to do in these pages.

In practicing then it behooves us to take advantage of what artists throughout the ages have known, and scientists have proven in their studies of the brain: *emotions and memories are bound together in the learning process.* Arundhati Roy, author of *The God of Small Things,* describes a young girl's exuberance at returning to the movie theatre to see her beloved, *Sound of Music*: "Smells, like music, hold memories. She breathed deep, and bottled it up for posterity."

Let's discuss some implications these premises hold for your practicing.

Picture yourself about to sit down to practice when the phone rings. Your mind starts racing: "It's okay to get this call, I haven't started practicing yet. I won't answer any more calls. But actually I did promise myself I'd use this hour just for practicing. The machine will pick it up and I'll call back later…but, suppose it's Marlene? We've been playing phone tag for days and…" Well, you get the idea.

We're all familiar with the process of *focus interruptus*. We've put our mind on one thing and another immediately beckons. Which is what often happens when we play and get interrupted by a sound in the audience, an internal thought, a missed note. Now what options do you have when your focus simultaneously pulls you north and south?

Let's look at three possible options.

1. The first option entails actually changing the situation. Answering the phone, in this case. That one is relatively simple (unless it leads you to further distractions). You eliminate the competing focus in your pathway, clearing the path so you can proceed with clear mind and relaxed body.

2. The second option entails changing your belief about the situation. You think, for example, "Yes, I'm dying to get the phone, but even if it's important I can always call back later. Right now I'm practicing and that's that!" Then you continue as you did with the first option. This time, instead of clearing the pathway by eliminating the distraction, you do so by placing it to the side of the pathway, knowing you can come back later and pick it up. Again, you proceed with clear mind and relaxed body.

    But, suppose your thoughts about the same situation sound like this: "That was probably Marlene—she'll be mad because she needs the information I have. She gets mad so easily—she'll probably hold this against me for days."

    Imagine the impact of that thought on your practicing. You may continue on your path and practice, but rather than sit on the side of the path, the distraction will undoubtedly roll down the middle of the path where you will continue to stumble over it. Your mind is pre-occupied, focus goes in and out, your forehead is knotted and stomach somewhat queasy. You may breathe shallowly and not even know it.

    The examples in the second option remind us that the thoughts we "speak" to ourselves, the *interpretations* we consciously or unconsciously make of situations, effect changes in our bodies and subsequently in our ability to focus. Our thoughts affect the way we practice just as they affect us throughout our daily lives.

3. The third option entails mentally transforming yourself, thereby eliminating the effects of the distraction on you. Using your focus and senses, you create your own separate pathway, unobstructed by distraction. Marlene, the call, your thoughts may still hover in the air, but they're on a parallel path that doesn't intersect yours.

The third option represents the mechanism performers need to master. When intruding thoughts or external events clutter your mind and challenge your focus, you the performer, whether at home or in the recital hall, need to know how to clear your pathway and let go of the anxious, emotional fall-out that ensues. You need to know how to then replace it with a non-threatening focal point which allows you to re-focus on the music. It's like putting your car in neutral before changing gear.

When intruding thoughts ("I hope I don't make a mistake") or external events (a cough, a paper rustling in the audience while you perform) deflect concentration, your mind and body need the means to react immediately and automatically to shift you to neutral, that is, to "calm," rather than to either of two stress-related modalities: running to your brain and obsessively talking to yourself, or rapidly descending into your body and panicking. Both of these states take you away from performing with ease. In the following pages you learn simple exercises giving you mastery to avoid the stress-related zones.

The need to know how to shift to neutral, that is to respond automatically with calm, is especially acute during that tiny, anticipatory moment when the following occurs very rapidly:

- You receive sensory input: for example, you hear someone coughing, or see someone in the audience yawn.
- You interpret the input: "My playing is boring that person (and probably everyone else)."
- Your body responds: it gets tense, palms may get clammy, your muscles work harder. You begin to make mistakes, which then feed back into the sensory loop: "Mistakes! Now I'm going to forget what comes next. Where am I?" You're responding to fear, and the body is getting ready to flee.

It is into that split-second moment between input and interpretation that the intervention of a calming response must be spliced. You are about to learn the steps to become the splicing master.

Part I

PREPARATION

Planning before work protects you from regret.

Inscription on a X Century Islamic ceramic bowl,
Metropolitan Museum of Art, New York

CHAPTER 1.

The Automatic Relax Response

If you keep your body relaxed,
the body is in contact with the
depths of your soul…is that clear?
Because it's quite important.

Pianist Claudio Arrau

The first step in the art of passionate practicing is learning to relax and clear the mind. You may already be familiar with relaxation techniques from breathing exercises, meditation, yoga, biofeedback, or stress reduction. The simple exercise in this chapter may sound familiar, but since it is the foundation for the entire technique you will master, go through the steps carefully without skipping any. You will use it throughout the book. As each step is part of a seamless learning process, it is important to go through them thoroughly in sequence.

Relaxation is so important because it helps keep us grounded in the present, rather than distracted by the past or worried about what might happen in the future. We need to learn this relax response because human beings are by nature programmed to worry about the future. "The brain is an anticipation machine, constantly planning for the future. If we can anticipate the future, we're more likely not to be eaten," declared the wise and humorous neurobiologist, Dr. Daniel Siegel, author of *The Developing Mind.*

And indeed, music *is* about anticipation, about long musical lines, about the overall architecture and design of each piece. As with speaking or dancing, music is about flow, seamless integration of past, present and future. It is only when anticipation gets aligned with worried thoughts or negative physical response that the need for grounding in the present becomes imperative. Musicians need to be able to detach themselves from past and future moments if necessary, so a glitch in bar 17 doesn't lead to glitches in bars 18 and 19.

Having a relaxed body and clear mind sounds good. Yet getting there can be a challenge. *Don't tell me to relax; it's my tension that holds me together* states a postcard I used to have tacked to my bulletin board. In today's stressful world it's no surprise people carry stress as naturally as they carry their books and briefcases. Holding stress over a long period of time often results in having one's stress feel natural—not one's breathing and relaxation. Full, rather than shallow breathing may even feel slightly risky since it makes us more present and visible. But present and visible also means connected and dynamic, and how become passionate—about music, about life—without such connection?

In addition to the sheer joy of having one's power released, I've witnessed a diversity of responses from students while they became relaxed. Sandra, a woman with extreme tension throughout her body had two fascinating responses when she released tension from her shoulders. First, she discovered that, since her tension had undoubtedly been holding her together, her body needed to discover how to be genuinely comfortable when more relaxed. This took time and experimenting with chairs, height, ways of sitting. Then, the sound on the keyboard that her easier arm/hand made was so full and rich that it frightened her at first. Perhaps this sounds strange to you, but Sandra had been used to sounding small, and a powerful sound suddenly made her feel bigger. She needed time to absorb this new aspect of herself. Little by little the exhilaration of coming into her own sound, as musician and as woman, overcame the strangeness and she has since become a passionate musician, a dynamic woman. She succeeded in creating a whole new image of herself.

Let's turn now to gently releasing your own power with easy, energy-enhancing exercises, beginning with ones that barely take any energy at all.

In the integrated method ahead you will be asked to do some exercises both at and *away from* your instrument. There are several reasons for doing exercises away from your instrument. First, it is often easier and more natural—like walking. You have more flexibility—more space, more opportunities for exploration, more room to move. Second, it momentarily detaches the exercise from the instrument so it can be enjoyed for its own sake, and not be burdened with thoughts connected to actual playing.

And thirdly, like the creative person you are becoming (and can read about in the *Coda*), it gives you an opportunity to see how just noticing experiences away from the instrument can enhance your music-making at the instrument. If you find you have difficulty going through any exercise, be patient with yourself and just play around with the ideas instead. You will be coming back to them as the ideas presented become increasingly integrated into your practice. For now, absorb what you can, read the rest for ideas, and be open to change.

You begin by practicing the following simple exercise away from the instrument. *Practice until it becomes an automatic response.*

THE CALMING LIGHT (sitting away from your instrument)

Sit in a comfortable chair with your feet unfolded and touching the floor, hands gently placed in lap. It's a good idea to have your mouth slightly ajar to relax your jaw, which is essential.

Now, simply put your awareness on your breathing, and breathe naturally. You can let your eyes close for now, though eventually you will do this exercise with eyes open, staying connected to your surroundings.

As you ride your breath, let your internal awareness follow the air as it gently passes through your slightly open mouth, your throat, trachea, into your chest, and down into your abdomen. Feel your waist expanding and contracting with your breathing. Watch your breathing as it travels this unobstructed road between your mouth and your abdomen. Continue to breathe easily as you follow the next step.

PRACTICING THE CALMING LIGHT RELAX RESPONSE, AWAY FROM YOUR INSTRUMENT

LIGHTING THE CALMING LIGHT: Your internal image.

Picture a point of light at a spot in your abdomen and watch yourself breathing *to* that spot, lighting it up. (If another image comes up for you, that's fine. Students have had success with various images including a candle, a calm lake, a shiny green stone.) Your image eventually becomes your cueing device, directly leading—cueing—you to calmness.

Let thoughts pass through as you continue to keep awareness on your breathing. Simply watch the thoughts as they occur. You can then put them in cartoon-like balloons and let them drift up and away. Or let them float away on drifting clouds. The important ones will return so you needn't worry about losing any. *If you find yourself engaging with any of these thoughts that's okay for now too.* But you will continue to consciously bring yourself back to your point of light in the center of your belly, and continue breathing naturally, even if your thoughts linger.

Remember, you are a complex being which means you can be aware of your thoughts *and* continue to keep awareness on your breathing. This is the first step in gaining control over your focus. With practice and future exercises you will find it easier to disengage, disconnect, ignore, and finally release yourself from interfering thoughts.

As you continue breathing, notice your arms getting heavier as tension is released from your shoulders and neck. Notice also that your body is supported by the chair under you and the floor under your feet. You are grounding yourself in your breathing. Feel your spinal cord running the length of your back into the chair. Let yourself release into these supports. If at first you get very relaxed, that's okay. Better to start from a feeling of complete relaxation than hold any tension. Eventually you will breathe yourself into a relaxed *and* alert state, which will be referred to as "R/A."

Do this exercise in your comfortable chair three times a day for three days. Set your kitchen timer or pocket watch for three minutes each time.

1. Call your internal image to mind (the point of light, for example).
2. Breathe directly to your image, jaw released.
3. Keep your awareness on your breathing.
4. Notice your arms getting heavy in your lap, your body being supported by spine, chair, floor.
5. Allow whatever thoughts you have to come and go, keeping awareness on your breathing

THE CALMING LIGHT
(away from your instrument, during your normal activities)

Your next step will be using this Calming Light exercise at appropriate times throughout the day wherever you are. If you have been practicing this exercise with eyes closed, practice now keeping your eyes open. This prepares for a relaxed/alert state staying connected to your surroundings, and eventually to your music or other artistic endeavor.

For the next three days, three times a day, do the same exercise whenever you feel yourself getting frazzled, frustrated or flustered. Try it, for example, driving in traffic; speaking with someone who makes you nervous; not having an answer to your friend's question; making an important phone call; waiting in line. Immediately go to your internal image and let the rest of the exercise fall into place: *breathing, getting grounded in your body by feeling both your spine and the floor supporting you, your arms released of excess tension (even if you're holding something).* **You are learning to put your body at ease while staying connected to your environment.**

Once again, don't worry if thoughts rush in. You are working on training your body to respond quickly and automatically to potentially stressful situations. Your mind will eventually follow. But even if it doesn't, you will have sufficient ease in your body that your thoughts will not affect that ease.

Throughout this book, you will be using the Calming Light to cue yourself into a relaxed/alert or R/A stance. You have already mastered the means to do this.

Using the calming light to cue to R/A (the relaxed/alert state)

You immediately bring your internal image into focus, which is your cue.

At this cue your body automatically responds:

> Eyes stay open. Your jaw relaxes.
>
> Your awareness is on breathing directly to your internal image.
>
> Your arms become heavy as tension gets released from shoulders/neck.

You are now ready to practice using the Calming Light to cue to R/A at your instrument. While the piano is named during the following exercise, other instrumentalists will take their natural places, either standing or sitting, with their own instruments, as if you were going to practice. (And, if, for example, you are practicing to give a public speech, then stand on your podium.)

THE CALMING LIGHT (at your instrument)

1. Sit at your keyboard, or music stand. Always check the height of your bench as well as your distance from the keyboard. This ensures optimum playing comfort. For pianists, be sure that your arms and hands are parallel to the floor. Set the timer for three minutes.
2. Immediately use the Calming Light to cue yourself into R/A.
3. Focus on breathing to your light with easy mouth, eyes open. Take your time, until you feel yourself being held up by your bench and your arms lying heavily in your lap.
4. Put thoughts into their balloons and let them float away.
5. Stay there with your instrument until the timer goes off.

Once again, if you have trouble letting go of your thoughts, don't be concerned. If this is a new experience for you—and your thoughts—it will take practice. Remember you couldn't play your instrument, nor read or write before you were taught and then practiced what you were taught. So follow the guidelines for cueing yourself into R/A and watch how you progress.

The following is a story about a student whose tenacious negative thoughts and images seemed firmly entrenched. The student, however, faithfully continued to do the exercise. Then, at one lesson, something happened.

Charlotte, a fifty-year-old woman had been battling a multitude of internal judges all her life, including former piano teachers. They were constantly feeding her negative thoughts, which left her no faith she'd ever be able to play the way she wanted. During the R/A exercise one male figure from her life refused to be "floated" away. He stood his ground and harangued. "You can't play. You don't have enough talent. Why bother? You're wasting your time." As she continued to remain aware of her breathing, she continued to watch the figure haranguing. Suddenly she began to smile as the figure became wrapped in a formal British barrister's outfit, complete with robes and wig. She started laughing as he slowly dissolved from a formidable foe into an amusing caricature. He hovered still a while longer, but my student, continuing to breathe naturally into her light, was able to disengage enough to increasingly connect with her own body and sever the strength of the emotional connection to the figure.

There are times, of course, when images hold so much emotional energy and power over you that you need to confront the issues more directly. This is addressed in a later chapter. But, now, before going on to the next step, there are two points that bear repetition:

1. **Human beings are complex creatures.** We often hold two contradictory thoughts or feelings simultaneously with no effort. If you've ever told a friend you didn't mind her canceling your date while inside you felt that nagging twinge of disappointment, if you have chatted nonchalantly with your teacher or boss while privately experiencing nervousness and fear, then you have already mastered the complex art of simultaneously being aware of disturbing thoughts and not acting them out. Desensitization to phobias works along similar paths. People learn to relax, then are exposed to increasingly more uncomfortable experiences with the feared object. With increasing practice they still know how terrified they used to be, yet they no longer respond with fear. Learning how to breathe and relax helps put distance between stimulus and response. It is "neutral." That is what you will be doing with interfering thoughts that may arise during the music-making process.

2. **You can play with passion and be relaxed at the same time.** The following story addresses the issue of whether playing passionately is compatible with playing without unnecessary tension:

   My son recently competed for his black belt in the martial art of Tae Kwon Do. Testing takes place all afternoon with judges giving verbal feedback to the competitors as the exam progresses. The single most repeated word that afternoon from *all* the judges, during *all* the exams was: RELAX. "You're going to break the board. No problem—relax!" "You're only using 25 percent of your body potential because you're not relaxed." The words used next in frequency were, "easier," "lighter."

And yes, my son earned his black belt.

The relaxation mode is as true for playing an instrument as for Tae Kwon Do. Before each note, after each note, why hold unnecessary tension? It is in those tiny moments—those split-seconds—between notes, when our thoughts race, our anticipation mounts and tension finds its niche. Knowing how to cue yourself using the Calming Light exercise into R/A, is the first step in releasing yourself to maximizing your potential.

The important question of playing passionately while remaining in R/A is explored further in the chapter, *Where's The Expression?* (If you can't wait to read that chapter, go ahead and do so, but be sure to come back and pick up where you left off.)

The next chapter explores the realm in which artists dwell: the senses.

Chapter 2.

Preparing Your Senses

Listening to running water makes me a better calligrapher.

Sung Dynasty calligrapher

His sound had a light in it.

Wynton Marsalis on Louis Armstrong

You have learned and practiced the first crucial step in this integrated approach: relaxing your body while making your mind both quiet and alert. In this chapter, we turn our attention to the next crucial step: opening and enhancing sensory awareness. There are several reasons to do this as a musician and artist.

First, since we learn through our senses, the livelier and more receptive they are, the easier and more efficient the learning. Secondly, lively receptive senses provide us many possible connections to the music while playing and, as we will soon see, those connections can provide safety nets against anxiety while performing. Thirdly, the more sensual experience we bring to music-making, the richer and more colorful our playing. Just as the Sung calligrapher stated, *listening* to running water makes us better musicians.

How many different sensory experiences occur for you during any single activity in a day? For example, taking a shower, speaking with someone, driving? As you expand your sensory experience with your instrument you will be surprised at how your everyday experience expands as well. And conversely, as your everyday sensory experiences expands, so too does your musical artistry.

Learning, we've seen, is primarily accomplished through the senses, especially the auditory, visual and kinesthetic, or hearing, seeing and feeling senses. Input from our senses can be first filtered through our brain, for example, when we hear a sound and think "what a lovely bird." Or it can be transmitted directly into our visceral system, when we hear a sudden loud noise and immediately jump, startled. We learn over time through repetition and through intensity of experience. When we repeat a passage over and over, to quote Alexander

Libermann again, we make that passage permanent. At other times we learn from a single, intense experience—burning a hand on the stove; biting into something that tastes horrible.

Repetition or intensity can each generate learning. What if we harnessed *both* repetition *and* intensity to the learning process? We would be in a much better position to learn efficiently and permanently, and thereby to be free to experience the passion. It's important to remember that the brain itself, the part that accepts input, does not make distinctions between what you *ought to* be learning and *ought not to* be learning. Repetition and/or intensity simply lay the pathways for future memory and retrieval. Therefore, you must be sure that *the experience you are intensifying and repeating is exactly what you desire to make permanent.*

You're familiar with learning from repetition. Every time you say "please" and "thank you" represents the million times your parents said, "What's the magic word, dear?" Eventually "please" and "thank you" become automatic responses, and we learn to say those phrases, whether we mean them or not. (And when we say "thank you" for that present that has already been relegated to the darkest spot in the closet, we are exhibiting that complex human behavior of feeling one way and behaving another. Be glad you know how to do that already! It will come in handy later on.)

Intensity here applied to learning, involves having an experience on multilevels of our sensory systems, either simultaneously or in sequence: listening to and watching a scary movie, listening to a loved one's voice while looking at his or her picture. If we were to read a book aloud, write down key words or thoughts that popped up as we read, discuss that book with others and even, perhaps, dramatize it—how much more vivid the memory of that particular book will be compared with another silently read through once.

Learning music is no different. Leonard Bernstein demonstrated that principle so artistically in his Young People's Concerts. If you can, watch those old tapes (many public libraries own them) to see Bernstein incorporate sounds, pictures, movement, and even audience participation. He used anything that would bring to life and imprint the material he was discussing. He made up crazy Superman stories to music; he led the audience in singing the same notes over and over imitating brass, percussion, strings, woodwinds to demonstrate the various kinds of sound from which a composer can choose in orchestrating a symphony.

To learn a piece of music well, we must bring as many senses to the learning process as possible, simultaneously. Everyone has different sensory strengths; that is, you may have a stronger visual acuity than aural, and as a musician that may tie you more to the written page of music. Or you might be at your best when you see *and* feel. And that might make you a great sight-reader. Such disparities within individuals are normal. However, to the extent you can develop your senses more fully and *connect them to each other,* the more powerful your own experience and learning will become. So don't be discouraged if at first you find one exercise more challenging than another. Give them all your best, and then let yourself be surprised.

Here you start by learning to focus on each individual sense separately. In the following exercises, all done away from your instrument, you will take the same R/A, relaxed/alert stance you did with the Calming Light breathing exercise.

Focusing on Visual Input

For these exercises you'll need earplugs or cotton for your ears, something to cover your eyes, and a kitchen timer. Cue yourself into R/A and go through the following exercises:

1. Choose a pleasant spot for yourself. It can be outdoors or in a room of your home. Set your timer to five minutes and put in your earplugs.

    For the next five minutes, examine your surroundings visually as if you're seeing them for the first time. Imagine your eyes are enormous, and you're a detective looking for visual clues.

    Get up and move. Don't touch as you walk around, but notice everything you can: colors, especially the differences in shades of the same color (the green in the plants, the green in the rug, for example); textures; how everything relates visually.

2. Put your television on and turn off the sound. Watch for five minutes. (This is especially interesting if you watch something dramatic or scary.) How does watching people's body language affect you?

3. Take a walk, put your ear plugs in and become a detective again. NOTICE, NOTICE, NOTICE everything that you pass.

   When you finish the exercises, jot down as many visually descriptive words as you can. For example, dark, bright, shimmering, vibrant, jarring, luminous.

Focusing on Auditory Input

To focus on auditory input take your earplugs out and cover your eyes. Use the Calming Light exercise to cue yourself into R/A and try the following exercises.

1. If you sat in a room for the visual exercise, sit in the same room. Spend the next five minutes focused on the sounds around you. Imagine your ears are huge, they are detectives. Even if it's very quiet, listen attentively. Music, like life, is made up of sounds and silences. The quality and differences of silences—rests—is as important as the quality of the sounds. Listening to the stillness is as important as listening to the sounds that surround you.

2. Walk outdoors for five minutes, keeping your eyes down, not covered, or let someone lead you with your eyes closed. Or, you can try to de-focus your eyes as you walk, while putting your focus on your enormous ears and their aural input. It would be loveliest to do this exercise in a beautiful spot where your ears will be titillated by the sounds of nature!

3. Put the TV on and listen for five minutes with your eyes covered.

   When you finish, jot down any *auditory* type words that occur to you: sharp, clangy, soothing, melodious, harsh, strident, sweet.

Focusing on the Kinesthetic

"Kinesthetic" can refer to feelings, movement, body memory or body reactions. For our purposes, *kinesthetic* will refer to two different kinds of sensory functions: the external feelings in the arms and hands as they move, and the internal movement or sensations in the body evoked by playing the music.

The kinesthetic sense is probably the most important sense related to learning and memorizing, since emotions and memory are wired together in the brain. Studies are showing that holding and touching an infant is not only soothing and bonding, but facilitates brain connections necessary for learning. Nature champions touch and feel by making them essential for brain development. Thus what you experience in the body is what you are most likely to remember. Feeling your own loss of a beloved pet far better instructs you about loss than reading or hearing about it.

Often when we forget something on a conscious level our body retains its own memory on a kinesthetic level, separate from our awareness. This is true especially after a particular behavior has been repeated often, such as driving to a best friend's house. One day, your mind dreamily drifting, you arrive at your friend's house without remembering the drive over. In performance, if the mind goes "blank" the body can easily take over as long as the mind doesn't actively interfere, but just drifts off as it does when you daydream while driving. It is therefore essential for the performer, when the mind interferes, to know how to let the mind drift off and let the body take over. This is exactly how I managed to get through that recital I mentioned after having a memory slip soon after I began playing.

The first step toward attaining this ability to let the body go on "automatic" as the mind "takes a vacation" has already been accomplished by the Calming Light exercise which you are continuing to practice. Now we seek to become more aware of the kinesthetic sense so that mind and body are, as much as possible, in alignment with each other.

Cue yourself into R/A with Calming Light breathing, and do the following exercises:

1. Set your timer for five minutes. Walk around a room and *touch* everything you can. Experience the different textures, and let your fingers linger over the objects they touch. Notice any internal reaction to touching different objects.

2. Watch TV, first with earplugs for a few minutes, then with eyes covered for a few minutes, and finally with eyes and ears open, and pay attention to the different internal reactions.

3. Speak with a friend on the phone and put your focus on the different feelings you go through during the entire conversation. Then do the same next time you talk with someone in a distinctly different relationship to you, like a parent, teacher, employer, store clerk. Just notice how those experiences differ for you.

Now jot down *feeling* words, both for the sensations you felt when *touching* something (rough, silky, hard, smooth, thorny, nubby) and when *feeling* something internally (happy, excited, angry, light-hearted, disappointed, melancholic).

You need to be able to switch from one sensory function to another with ease, so use any of the above exercises, or make up your own to practice. And you may want to practice the most on the sense that felt weakest in order to more fully develop it. Eloise Ristad, author of *Soprano on Her Head,* used to have members of her workshops play ball together, instructing them first to simply toss the ball, then *watch* the ball as it flew in space, then *listen* to it as it hit their hands, then *feel* it as it entered their hands. It was always eye-opening to experience how much more focused people became, and at the same time, how much their "performance" of catching the ball improved, when the focus was on a sense perception and not on catching. Sports coaches know this method well.

By now you have experienced and begun gaining ease and comfort with the two vital techniques upon which the integrative method of practicing is built: using the Calming Light to cue yourself into R/A, and switching your focal awareness among sensory channels. Practice these skills until they are automatic.

You are almost ready to sit with your instrument and put into practice all that you have already learned. But first let me invite you to enjoy some useful techniques that will make the entire learning process more effortless. Indeed, they are techniques based on natural movements you use daily that I invite you to bring to your music-making.

Then, in Part II you will put all that you learned so far into making music with your instrument.

CHAPTER 3.

Magic Carpet, Puppy Dog Hands and Creating a Partnership with Your Instrument

A mind free to respond cannot help doing two things to
whatever confronts it; it connects and it animates.

The Seamless Web, Stanley Burnshaw, poet and author

You now know how to clear your mind and bring yourself into your body.

You now know how to place your sensory focus where you want: on listening, seeing, or feeling.

Those are the essential tools for mastering learning and performing.

But before you put those together in your own practice, I'd like you to look at several additional components critical to effortless playing. I call them:

1. The Magic Carpet
2. The Puppy Dog Hand
3. The Animated Instrument

These particular exercises are addressed to the pianist but are easily transposed for any instrument. When the pianist, for example, places her hands on the keyboard, you, violinist, guitarist, harpist, will reach for your own instrument and get your hands in position to practice as well. When she plays or explores her instrument, you naturally do the same with yours. As each concept is discussed, I hope you'll enjoy discovering their benefits while also enjoying doing the exercises. Again, take your time. Let yourself be fanciful. Let yourself be surprised.

The Magic Carpet (sitting next to your instrument)

"The Magic Carpet" conjures up fairy tales and fantasy. It is Aladdin freely floating on a wavy Disney colored cloth, propelled across the sky by the magic power upon which he sits. Here we borrow some magic power to bring increasing ease to playing. This is how it works.

THE MAGIC CARPET
HOLDING YOUR ARMS UP

When you cue yourself with Calming Light into R/A, your arms and hands become heavy. Weight falls into them from your shoulders. Now, instead of consciously working to lift them to the keyboard, imagine a magic carpet or cushion, called on command to fly under each arm and gently lift both arms up from your lap and onto the keyboard.

It may help to imagine a golden triangle that begins with your Calming Light breathing. Watch yourself inhale to your point of light, and at the same time let that inhalation lift your arms up. That is equivalent to the magic carpet lifting your arms. As you exhale, you also exhale your arms down onto the instrument. You exert no effort—your arms are literally transported for you by your breathing, which serves the same function here as the magic carpet.

Once onto the keyboard, continue to feel the gentle support of the billowy carpet under your arms. Notice how little energy it actually takes to keep your arms in position. Paradoxically, as you continue to feel the weight in your arms, you feel they are light enough to remain in position by themselves. It is akin to floating on water, as your relaxed heavy body is buoyed gently up by the water alone, not by its own effort. It is the feeling captured in the following poem, *'The Avowal'* by Denise Levertov:

> *As swimmers dare*
> *to lie face to the sky*
> *and water bears them,*
> *as hawks rest upon air*
> *and air sustains them*
> *so would I learn to attain*
> *freefall, and float*
> *into Creator Spirit's deep embrace,*
> *knowing no effort earns*
> *that all-surrounding grace.*

The Magic Carpet (at the keyboard, at your instrument)

Cue yourself into an R/A state. Feel the heaviness in your arms, waiting as long as you need for all the weight to fully descend into them. Now without lifting them yourself, imagine the carpet gliding under your arms and lifting them over the piano. Continue to feel the carpet supporting your arms and the minimal amount of energy it takes to keep your arms afloat at the keyboard.

The Magic Carpet (away from your instrument)

Exercises to help the body understand the feeling:

1. Stand in place and let your arms hang down. Breathe into your feet. Then, simply walk, and let your arms swing naturally, feeling the ease with which they move.
2. Get a friend, or take a child and go outside and toss a ball around. Notice the freedom with which you toss the ball from your shoulder, and look at your hand as it comes back into a relaxed position immediately upon releasing the ball.
3. Next time you take a bath or swim, put your awareness on the buoyancy of the water, and on how your body feels as it is kept afloat.

The Puppy Dog Hand

When your arms are heavy, or after you release a ball, or when you let your hands fall easily, palm up, in your lap, there is no extra tension in your hands. They look like a puppy dog's paws when she's on her back waiting to get a tummy rub. All easy and floppy. This is "home" position for your hands, the feeling they return to automatically—after some practice—between notes, immediately after playing a note, even while holding a note. You are increasingly becoming aware of how you hold tension in your hands on gross and subtle levels, at and away from your instrument. This tension plays a big role in escalating anxiety once tension kicks in.

PUPPY DOG DEMONSTRATING PUPPY DOG HANDS

The Puppy Dog Hand (at the keyboard)

1. Cue yourself into R/A. Give yourself plenty of time.

2. Your arms rest in your lap, palms up. Wait for them to get heavy. Slowly roll arm and hands over, palms facing down.

3. Feel the Magic Carpet glide under your arms, lifting your arms over the keyboard. Notice them as they gently descend onto the keys, keeping your hands in exactly the same Puppy Dog position they were in on your lap. In other words, don't anticipate by spreading your fingers into any particular position as they descend onto the keyboard, or around your instrument. Even if your five fingers only cover a few notes, simply place them on the keys.

4. As the Carpet continues to support your arms, notice *the minimum amount* of energy you need to keep them at the keyboard.

5. Practice raising and lowering your arms keeping your hand in Puppy Dog position as the hand is lowered onto the keyboard and raised above it. Be sensitive to the slightest intrusion of tension into any part of your hand—by *watching* your hand closely, and by being in touch *kinesthetically*. The visual *and* kinesthetic components reinforce each other so that you can tell, by looking or feeling, whether your hand is relaxed or not.

THE MAGIC CARPET LIFTING THE PUPPY DOG HAND TO YOUR INSTRUMENT

Now you are ready to practice "traveling," that is, effortlessly going from one note or chord to another along the keyboard. Your mode of transportation is the Magic Carpet, and your traveling hand is in Puppy Dog position. No suitcase, no unnecessary baggage for this travel.

Once again from your lap, let the Carpet raise and deliver your heavy arms to the keyboard. As your fingers descend in Puppy Dog position upon the keys, let the weight in your arms, aided by gravity, lower your fingers into the key bed where they play whatever notes they fall on. Immediately release back into Puppy Dog. (Remember the feeling of release after tossing a ball.) Let the ever-ready Carpet quickly glide under your arms and transport you to another spot on the keyboard where you repeat the action of playing and simultaneously releasing into Puppy Dog.

MAGIC CARPET AND PUPPY DOG AT A GLANCE

1. Arms heavy in lap. Hands in Puppy Dog.
2. Magic Carpet glides under and picks heavy arms up and to keyboard.
3. When hands are on keyboard, supported by the Magic Carpet, the arms borrow energy from the internal weight to remain there. The rest of the weight plus gravity combine to let the hands/arms fall onto the notes and into the key bed.
4. As the notes get played the hand simultaneously releases into Puppy Dog.

In your daily life, notice how tightly you hold your hands, especially when:

1. Writing
2. Driving
3. Washing dishes
4. Brushing your teeth
5. Gardening
6. Holding the telephone

What happens when you begin to notice how you hold your hands throughout the day during normal activities? What effect does your noticing hand tension have on your shoulder/neck/jaw tension?

Carol-Ann, a young woman who took my first workshop "Problem-Solving for Pianists," at University of California, Berkeley Extension, spoke about pains she experienced in the upper part of her body. As I questioned her, she realized she experienced these pains not only while playing the piano, but throughout the day as well. I asked her what she did.

"I'm a lab technician."

Her homework assignment was simply to notice how she handled the lab equipment while doing her job. We didn't discuss the matter again for the next few weeks.

Towards the last session of the workshop, I asked her how her pains were. She looked puzzled for a moment, then said, "I just realized I'm not in pain anymore."

She had simply put her awareness on how she handled lab equipment, and as a result, had begun to automatically adjust the amount of energy she expended, thereby experiencing generalized relief almost immediately. Her experience reminded me of my own during the biofeedback sessions. Noticing, letting go, attaining freefall and floating as in Levertov's poem—all help the body attain ease.

Harriet, another young woman who had terrible fears about playing in public, became aware of how she clenched her jaw while playing. For her the mere releasing of the tension in her jaw muscles was enough to allay anxiety. She wrote me after playing successfully at her teacher's recital: "HOORAY. I got through. And I even felt good about my playing."

These stories illustrate how attention to areas of the body can be beneficial in alleviating stress. Awareness is often the first step in the process of lessening stress and pain.

CREATING A PARTNERSHIP: Animating Your Instrument

Children's chess coach Norman Alston tells young chess players:

If you're really quiet, you can hear the
(chess) *pieces shouting at each other. Then*
(you) *understand there's something really*
exciting going on. These pieces aren't inanimate.

I love feet. They talk to me. As I take them in my
hands, I feel their strengths, their weaknesses.
Salvatore Ferragamo, the famed shoemaker.

Instruments other than the piano get held, hugged, caressed and danced with. Picture the oboe or sax—up in the air they are swung. The violin and viola—lovingly enveloped by neck-chin-cheek and arms. The cello—locked in a leg embrace while caressed across its body. The harpist and harp in continual body contact. "He did not play the violin, he became the violin," said Bruno Walter of the immortal Fritz Kreisler.

Become the piano? Too big, too clumsy. A monster to conquer, make peace with, but not befriend. Constantly being worked on instead of with. It gets hit from above while we, students of the keyboard, are cajoled to "imitate the sweetness of the violin," "play deeply, richly—like a cello," "make the piano sing." It was to hear vocal artists that Chopin sent his piano students to understand beautiful sound. When the metaphor revolves around struggle, then stress and strain aren't far behind. It is time to change the metaphor, the attitude with which the entire piano-playing process is imbued, and notice the impact such a change in attitude effects.

Suppose your best friend calls to say he needs to talk with you. If you're feeling badly about something you said that may have hurt his feelings, you can imagine how your mind and body will react to thought of the impending talk. Knowing, however, that he needs your help planning a surprise party for your mutual friend will assuredly elicit a different response.

Let's do the same shifting of gears with your instrument. In the following short section, you will do a different kind of exercise than those in the rest of the book. Most exercises entail following small step-by-step instructions. However, in this particular exercise, you participate in a mental shift in order to consider the relationship between you and your instrument a partnership, not a conflict. To make that shift, we look to Burnshaw's lovely quote at the beginning of this chapter as guide, for you will need *a mind free to respond* in order to **connect with** and then *animate,* your instrument. There is then, between you and your instrument, a dynamic interplay, rather than a need to dominate over an inanimate, adversarial object.

A child-like curiosity is ideal, as we begin with an old fairy tale.

CREATING A PARTNERSHIP (at the piano, at your instrument)

Remember the story of the blind men and the elephant? There were seven blind men who had never seen the massive animal and wished to determine the essential qualities that make an elephant an elephant. Each stood at a different spot near the elephant, and soon came to his individual conclusion. One declared the elephant very much like a snake, because he held the tail. Another declared the elephant like the trunk of a tree—he was next to a foot.

Well, for a moment let yourself become all the blind men in order to get a full feeling for the piano-animal. After clearing your piano of anything on or around it and clearing your mind to enjoy a child-like curiosity, pretend you have no idea what a piano is or does, and have been sent on a mission to uncover its essential qualities. All you have been told is that it is a living entity of unknown purpose.

Taking your time, and alternating with eyes open and shut, slowly run your hands over its exterior. *Feel* the difference between the different materials of this animal: wood, ivory, plastic, steel. *Look* carefully inside, and underneath, if it's a grand. *Listen* while you experiment making different sounds all over your instrument. In other words, like the blind men, find as many facets of this "animal" as you can, as if you had no preconceived notion what it sounds like nor what, if any, are its limitations. As you walk around feeling and listening, you'll also *look* at each area of this new creature, and then at its entire being.

With both hands touching your instrument, close your eyes and get a sense of its "being"—does it feel masculine or feminine? young or old? responsive to your touch? Staying in contact and, with eyes closed and hands still touching, ask it a ques-

TICKLING MORE
THAN THE IVORIES

45

tion, and allow yourself to "intuit" its answer. Let yourself be surprised. Tell it a secret and let it respond. Now—slowly—with hands still on the piano, guide yourself over to the keyboard and sit down. Or get yourself in position with your instrument to play.

Sitting at the keyboard. As the Magic Carpet lifts and lowers your hands onto the keys, close your eyes and feel the response of the keys under your fingers. With a 'mind free to respond,' animate the keys, feel their buoyancy, feel the different sensations in your fingertips as you try different touches and dynamic variations—moderately loud *legato*, brilliant *staccato*, soft *detached*, clear *pointed* sound. Become familiar with the interplay between the sounds produced and the resulting feelings or vibrations in your fingers, arms, and especially body. In other words, start becoming aware of the give-and-take of the musical dance between yourself and your instrument.

This is a wonderful way to begin a performance when you have to play on a totally different piano than the one you're used to. Instead of regarding it with trepidation, not knowing how it will respond once you start playing, take a few moments to put your hands on it (even if only mentally as you sit with the audience focused on you), connect with it, animate it. Become partners.

CREATING A PARTNERSHIP (away from your instrument)

Gather together some drawing paper and colored felt pens or pencils. For a week, take a few minutes each day before practicing and draw a different picture of your instrument. Don't worry about being realistic or artistic, and certainly do not be judgmental: the freer the better. The idea is not to make a perfect copy of your instrument, but to give visual expression to your internal feelings about it. Use your imagination and put each picture in a different context so that you wind up with seven different versions of your 'piano studies.'

If you can, tape them up around the wall, or just keep them together nearby where you can spread them all out in front of you. Stand back and look at them. What do they tell you about your relationship with your instrument? Were there any surprises? If so, what?

Now *animate* the pictures by letting each one "speak" to you—let words or phrases pop out at you as you study each one. Find out how your instrument responds to having been drawn, to the different contexts, to differing versions of itself.

Finally, what is it like for you to be thinking of your piano or flute in this way, away from the actual instrument?

What you have done in the above exercises is to slow down to become aware of and focus on your relationship with your partner in music-making. If previously this relationship had been one of benign neglect, dominance, fear, anything other than mutual respect and love, it's time to put those old feelings into perspective and create room for a new one.

Using the Calming Light, cue yourself into the R/A state. As you continue to keep awareness on breathing easily, let any old, negative words and thoughts associated with your instrument come into focus *(it's too hard, I'll never be good, my sister's so much better, etc)*.

Patiently, staying inside your body through your breathing, watch each idea get lighter and lighter until it floats away. (It is important to let them float away in as detached a way as possible, not vengefully or hatefully.) Send them to "old, no-longer-useful-idea" heaven, where they can comfortably rest, no longer needing to return to interfere.

Congratulations. It is very impressive to see what you have accomplished so far:

EVERYTHING YOU LEARNED SO FAR AT A GLANCE

1. How to use Calming Light to cue yourself into a relaxed state, anywhere you are: internal image, breathing, relaxed jaw—any of these can trigger the R/A state.
2. How to release tension in your body by letting the weight drop into your arms.
3. How to stay relaxed while letting thoughts drift up, even as you are aware of them.
4. How to focus on your different sensory channels.

In Part II you put everything you have mastered so far into practice with the music you are working on. You are approaching the point where the learning process becomes increasingly seamless and integrated.

Part II

PRACTICE

Piano practice is the best way
I know to feel organized.

Little Altars Everywhere

CHAPTER 4.

Breathing with the Music

In Part II you put all that you have already mastered—calming mind and body, and sensory awareness—into practice for optimum learning and performing. This chapter begins that process by showing you how to incorporate the Calming Light-Relaxed/Alert exercise into your practicing. From now on, think of yourself as the teacher, training mind and body in the responses necessary for learning and performing.

When you incorporate the R/A state from the first stages of practicing, it becomes the *default* position. This is vital when you experience distraction. Since you want the R/A stance to automatically replace anxiety as a reflex response, you must spend the necessary time teaching it to your body, and, like any good teacher, you must have lots of patience. You will realize the benefits accruing from this state after you have integrated it fully.

Read the whole chapter first before practicing the exercises, to become familiar with them and make sure you understand them. If you are, for example,

RELAXED/ALERT AT YOUR INSTRUMENT

ple, a singer, woodwind or brass player, think what adjustments you'll make in your breathing while singing or playing. Then go through the chapter step by step. Your goal is to learn how to incorporate the R/A stance from the first moment of learning a piece.

Choose a short, relatively easy piece of music to do this exercise, for example a Bach minuet. Most of the time will be spent *in-between* playing, not actually playing.

1. Sit comfortably, checking for height of chair and posture.

   Cue yourself into the R/A state, with your eyes open. (From now on, whenever you cue into R/A, keep your eyes open.)

   Feel your internal connection by breathing to your point of light, or other image, and feel your spine going directly into the chair, your feet supported by the floor, your arms in your lap.

   Stay alert and eager, aware of the surrounding environment, but detached from it because you are attached to your breathing.

2. Watch the Magic Carpet bringing your hands to the keyboard and placing them in Puppy Dog position on the keys.

3. Play only the first bar of the piece *plus* the following downbeat. Then STOP.

4. Magic Carpet your hands back into your lap, and cue yourself back into R/A, taking as long as you need until you are completely back into awareness of your breathing, arms heavy.

5. When you are completely back to R/A, that is, awareness off the music and back onto your breathing with arms relaxed, play the second bar, starting with the downbeat (even if it's a rest) and go to the next bar's downbeat. STOP and come back to R/A.

6. Repeat Step 4. Then, do this for only a few more bars, one bar at a time so that you don't get bored, or lose ability to concentrate.

7. Take a break and move around, or do something totally unrelated.

8. When you come back, you will repeat the exercise. Instead of stopping and cueing to R/A after *one* bar + 1 beat, you do so after *two* bars + 1 beat. The important thing is not to begin the next segment of music until you have completely come back to R/A.

9. Once again after a short break, do the exercise by playing *four* bars + downbeat at a time, in-between cueing to R/A.

10. Next go through the entire piece in R/A, and stop only if you lose your R/A state. At that point, put your hands in your lap and cue yourself back.

This last step is the connective link to actual performance and should only be tried when you are convinced you have done the preceding steps completely and honestly. Your goal is to play through the entire piece in R/A without stopping. If you lose focus, cue yourself back to R/A *while continuing to play.* If you were unable to continue playing in R/A, simply go back to the last successful step you completed and work your way down again. Be patient, and give yourself time between steps.

When you have successfully completed the last step, congratulate yourself. You have moved forward one giant step towards the ultimate goal of becoming a more fully integrated musician who can play with security and confidence.

You should practice this "breathing with your music" exercise for five minutes every day, each time with a different section of music that you are learning. In the chapter, Changing the "Uh-Oh" Mind-Set, you will see how useful it is with hard-to-play and hard-to-memorize spots.

The next chapter will lead you through the steps needed to enlist your sensory channels as safety nets in the learning process.

CHAPTER 5.

The Eight-Point Sensory System

Your focus determines your reality.

Qi-Gon to Anakin Skywalker, Star Wars, Episode 1

In this chapter your mind and body gain additional tools, vastly expanding how you flex the same sensory muscles with which you automatically learn in the first place. This reinforces and intensifies your learning. This sensory system should also be used in conjunction with other methods of learning, such as harmonic analysis, you may already be employing.

You have already identified the three primary sensory avenues of input: auditory, visual, and kinesthetic. I break those down even further to get a sense of how many avenues arc actually at your disposal in learning music:

AURAL

1   The sound of the music
2   The sound of your spoken voice
3   The sound of your internal voice

VISUAL

4   The written music
5   The keyboard
6   Your hands

KINESTHETIC

7   The movement in your arm/hand
8   The internal body feeling or gesture

This will be referred to as **The Eight-Point Sensory System.**

You may wonder at including the sound of your internal voice in the sensory system, rather than as part of your thought process. There are several reasons for doing so. To begin with, much of what we tell ourselves originated as aural input—someone said something to us—and was then internalized. Most likely it became exaggerated and invested with emotional associations. Think back on a time when someone said something to you about your music-making that had an adverse effect on you. For example: "If you only had the talent your sister had." "Don't you hear your mistakes?" "If you don't practice more you can't have lessons." "Hmmm. What an odd interpretation." Take time now to jot down anything negative from your own past that got stuck in your internal auditory system.

You may very well have also gotten plenty of positive feedback in your life. Take some moments to recall and list all the positive feedback you have gotten. Be careful not to dismiss those comments as less important, or as "they were just being nice to me" comments. Hold onto both lists for now. You can add to them as you remember other feedback that affected your music-making process. Later on you will have the opportunity to decide how you'd like to treat these lists.

Why is it that we so often tend to give more power to the negative than the positive comments? And why is it that those are the ones that often get lodged in our brain, usually with their very own microphone to our internal ear?

Perhaps you heard disparaging remarks enough times for them to become part of your own belief system. You begin to feed yourself such remarks, at which point you not only *hear* them internally, and *feel* the emotional effect they produce, but you also make a cognitive interpretation about them, sometimes without realizing it: "It's true, I'm not as talented as my sister…I probably shouldn't be playing; why am I wasting my time…" "My interpretation is probably wrong. Maybe I'm really not musical."

There are two elements involved in the internal voice: what you hear internally, and what you think about what you're hearing. Sometimes we know intellectually that the words we hear internally are not accurate. "Hey, wait a minute—I'm much *more* talented than my sister!" "I love playing; this isn't a waste of time." "There's nothing wrong with my interpretation." Despite that, the criticism may be lodged in the body separately from the corrective thoughts you know to be true.

To the extent you treat unwanted thoughts *as if* they were the same as hearing the dog bark, car honk, or someone coughing—that is, as simple sensory input which doesn't trail a lot of emotion behind it—the more control you will gain over managing your focus, concentration and energy. By depriving your internal thoughts of their emotional intensity you *de-toxify* their effect on you. The exercises in this book, geared toward relaxing your body and giving you control to release the connection between you and your thoughts, are expressly designed for that purpose.

When your thoughts are so invested with emotion that they cannot be treated as part of the sensory system, it's time to approach them with a different kind of care. We turn to that in the *Coda: The Passionate Performer.*

Let's return to The Eight-Point Sensory System. The more channels in the system you cultivate, the more efficient your learning and the more safety nets you have while performing.

To illustrate the ideas in putting the Eight-Point Sensory System to work, we'll use the Chopin Prelude in E Minor. **(See music.)** Afterwards, you can apply these principles to a piece you are currently studying. If you are not a pianist, you may still recognize this famous piece. In any case, read through the following steps and you will learn how to use the Eight-Point Sensory System for yourself.

Before reading a piece through for the first time, it is a good idea to gain some familiarity with it. Listen to a recording, but only once or twice to leave room for your own interpretation. Next, as you visually notice basics such as key and time signature, say them out loud as well: "E MINOR; 2/2—CUT TIME." This way you'll immediately begin practicing using two sensory channels. (Remember, this is a practice demonstration. You will revise later as you get proficient.)

Speaking of speaking out loud: those of us *of a certain age* constantly struggle with memory. We spend a lot of time going from room to room looking for that book, that

Repeating out loud helps you remember

55

Chopin, Prelude in E Minor

pen, or… I can't remember what else. Often, not only have we forgotten where we put the article, but what it was we were looking for when we entered the room. One device that has cut down enormously on my own search time is saying exactly what I'm looking for *out loud* as soon as the search begins. I repeat, "green sweater, green sweater," a few times going from room to room. This has greatly cut down on time expended searching for things, and leaves me that much more time for practicing.

Back to the music. Glance through the music and notice musical patterns. Immediately your eye corroborates what your ear heard: that the piece is in two parts, the second part opening with the same theme as the beginning (bar 13). Chances are you will now proceed to learn the piece by playing it through whatever number of times it takes to "get it." So let's jump ahead for a moment to that time when you first play it through without looking at the music.

Suppose you get to the return of the theme and mistakenly play bar 14 just like bar 2, realize your mistake, correct it and go on. Chances are you will continue to make that mistake, correct it and go on, since *practice makes permanent.* That is, unless you intervene.

The moment for intervening is *the very first time a mistake occurs.* That is the moment for perfect practicing, especially when you want to replace inaccuracy with accuracy. Since the brain learns with repetition, you want to be sure that what you repeat is what you want to make permanent.

When you find yourself doing something inaccurately: intervene right at the point where you want to substitute one learning for another, and in a calm state interject the desired set of auditory, visual and kinesthetic cues.

Here's how, step-by-step. (Remember whenever you play any of these exercises at your instrument to go from one note or chord to the next in Puppy Dog position, transported by the Magic Carpet.)

1. Cue yourself into R/A.

   Look at the spot on the page where you got derailed. Analyze exactly what the problem is: the chord change on the second beat in bar 14 differs slightly from the same spot in bar 2. Now taking each of those two spots you'll do a conscious comparison using all your sensory equipment, as follows. (Remember, we are using a simple example but the process applies to any music.)

2. Your body in R/A, your hands in Puppy Dog in your lap, let the Magic Carpet lift hands to the keyboard.

3. Fix in your eye the place on the page where each of these bars resides. Let's call the spot in Bar 2, the first time the harmonic change in question occurs, spot #1.

4. *Look* at spot #1. Play the chord, noticing it in any way that makes sense to you, for example: black keys on the outside, white in the middle. *Look* at how your hand looks sitting on that particular chord. Let your eye go back and forth between the exact spot on the page and your hand playing the chord.

5. *Feel* that particular chord in your hand so that the feeling in your hand coincides with the look of your hand playing *that* chord.

6. While *listening* carefully, play the progression from the immediately preceding chord to that chord, *looking* at the precise change: only the top note descends. Then *say* out loud any statement that makes sense to you, like 'top note only' or 'top note down.' *Feel* your hand as it makes this move from the first chord to the second in Bar 2, noting the very slight accommodation your hand actually makes for the thumb to physically go up a half-step from the white onto the black key. (The note itself descends a half-step, but your hand goes up to play it.)

7. In a completely relaxed state, simultaneously play this progression as you fix in your eye the spot on the page, *watching* the change on the keyboard, *saying* it out loud, *listening* to the sound, and feeling the movement the hand makes. (We will come back to internal feeling in a minute.)

Though it took you some minutes to read all those steps and go through them one by one, step #7 should take but a moment. It's the crowning moment of all the practice that went before.

Follow the above steps at spot #2, noticing and making the appropriate changes. For example, in step #6 you might say, 'outside notes both descend a half-step.' Or more simply, you might say 'one' for spot #1 with one change in the chord, and 'two' for spot #2 with the two changes. You will also notice how the hand moves somewhat more to accommodate the new angle in the chord at spot #2. You may also have experienced a more intense visceral response, a slight intake in the abdomen because of the intensity of the change. That too shall be used shortly in the learning process.

Remember, even with this kind of quality practice, there has to be quantity as well. Every step needs to be repeated so that not only are the right notes practiced into the fabric of the piece, but also the right body responses. Under duress the body reverts to old habits if new ones haven't become automatic. I call the number of repeats it takes for a passage to become automatic, the "magic number."

The 'magic number' is the number of times you practice a spot *after* getting it exactly the way you want it. It was said that for Horowitz the number was 100. For us more mortal pianists, perhaps it lies somewhere between 5 and 20. It is by practicing in a relaxed state, using all the sensory channels, and then "magic numbering" that you build in as solid a foundation of your music as possible.

It is time to add the essential ingredient of expressivity—musical meaning—into practice. Once again bear in mind that, despite the fact that these steps are introduced here in a linear, step-by-step process, with practice they become increasingly seamless and integrated. If the musical meaning is clear to you early in the stage of learning, it should be incorporated into this kind of practicing early in the process.

Incorporating that Crucial Kinesthetic Response

I always get in trouble with my friends when I go to concerts with them. Sated with the musical experience, they rave; left still hungry for something more, I sulk. We hear beautiful music, played carefully with a great deal of thought or with startling flare. Usually there are no glaring wrong notes or memory slips. It leaves me frequently dazzled, often jealous: such talent, dedication and success. But it hasn't moved me. And as a listener, I hunger to be moved by the music.

The exercises you have been practicing so far provide you with a means of making parts of the learning process automatic. Once they're automatic, you won't be thinking about them any more than you think how to drive your car or make a phone call. But knowing how to drive or use a phone is not the goal. Your goal is normally to get somewhere or speak with someone.

Likewise, your goal in playing is to make connections, first with yourself, then with your instrument, always with your music and finally, if you perform, with others. Your kinesthetic sense is the pathway to such connections. In this section, you begin making these connections and opening up your most passionate self.

Looking again at the "E Minor Prelude," you may already have an over-all idea of its character. But if you haven't heard it or formulated a feeling-picture of its intent, look for clues: the key of E minor; the words *Largo* and *espressivo* at the top; the descending melody over a persistent, incessant rhythm.

Within this framework and still concentrating on the practice spots, follow the steps below.

1. Play from the beginning to spot #1. Stop and immediately put your awareness on your internal feeling, your body's response to the music. You don't need words, just a sense of what happens internally at this musical moment.

    Play the same passage again, focused on your internal kinetic response. Then guarding this feeling internally, notice the external movement of your hands. Link the visual with the kinetic in your mind.

2. Go to spot #2, following the same progression. You've already noted the difference in the hand motions. Now add awareness of the difference in body response at spot #2.

    Now, get up and stand away from the keyboard. Don't take any time to think about the next steps, just do them as you read them.

3. Get into the internal state of spot #1, and let your body externalize that internal feeling by *becoming a statue of that feeling.* Let yourself be surprised at the outcome.

PUTTING INTERNAL MUSICAL FEELING INTO A STATUE POSE

Remaining in statue form, say out loud whatever word or phrase comes to mind.

4. Do the same for spot #2.

5. Close your eyes and, saying out loud whatever words came up at the two spots (let's say they were "pleading" and "yearning"), let your body go from statue #1 — "pleading" — to statue #2—"yearning"— intensifying and imprinting those statues viscerally into your system as you hear yourself repeating those key words.

   Exaggerate the motion and feelings. For example, if you feel an internal contraction in your stomach at spot #2 which sends your torso slightly up and forward, then exaggerate the contraction and upward/forward motion. After treating those spots with their rightful drama and implanting the drama into your body, it is unlikely you will forget them.

6. Go back to the keyboard, and cue into R/A. Say out loud: "one." Become statue #1, and play that passage. Connect your hand movements to your statue. Then switch and say out loud: "two" and become statue #2. "Magic number" those spots.

The next step is incorporating the sections back into the piece and playing the whole piece through without thinking of any of the learning mechanisms nor even feeling the slightest anticipatory cringe as you approach a well-worked section.

The Performance Situation

How do you use these techniques during a performance? What happens if while performing this piece you get a slightly anticipatory cringe as you approach spot #1 or #2? There are two ways to handle this situation in performance:

1. Immediately cue to R/A. Focus on breathing as your body automatically releases tension. Continue keeping your focus on breathing, and away from the music. This makes a momentary disconnect between your body and

mind before your thoughts spiral out of control and land you into one of the stress zones referred to earlier. Your body is now on automatic pilot. This is like you driving to your friend's house without knowing how you got there. Because you know this piece so well from having practiced in R/A using all sensory apparatus, you can trust your body to continue without your mind's involvement. Once calm, you can bring your awareness back on the music.

2. Cue to R/A and focus on the part of the Eight-Point Sensory System that is most helpful in bringing you back to the music:

    AURAL:
    • the anticipated *sound of the chord*
    • sound of your *spoken* verbal cue—now *internalized*, for example: "1 change" at spot 1, "2 changes" at spot 2

    VISUAL:
    • the written *page* (seen now in your mind's eye)
    • the notes on the *keyboard*
    • your *hands* as they move to the appropriate notes

    KINESTHETIC:
    • the kinesthetic feeling in your *hand*
    • the *internal* kinesthetic statue.

Either way will get you through that moment until you can ease yourself back into the flow of the music.

Before continuing, think about possible non-musical situations in which the mind-set created by the R/A-Eight-Point Sensory System could be beneficial to you. How can it be applied to sports; academic studies; entering a room full of strangers; making friends? Notice how you have already begun using that way of thinking in situations away from your instrument. Take a moment to write them down.

As the Jedi of your instrument, what kind of reality would you like to create for yourself and your instrument?

CHAPTER 6.

Changing the "Uh-Oh" Mind-Set

"Please, God, let me get through this next section," pleaded a dear friend silently while performing his senior recital at Juilliard. "If you do, I promise never to perform again." Few are the musicians who couldn't sympathize with such distress.

Was he prepared? Very. What went wrong? He can't recall. But it could be he stumbled on a spot in the music he'd once had problems with and practiced 'til blue in the face. And having given it so much attention, that spot achieved "uh-oh" status, as in: "Uh-oh, here comes that section." As a performer approaches such a section he feels tension rising, anxiety escalating, mind racing. Invariably, he begins to make mistakes.

However, in addition to making deals with the piano god or goddess, you can now use the tools you have been practicing. We take musical spots that trigger your "uh-oh" mind-set and saturate those spots with the R/A-Eight-Point Sensory System until "uh-oh" becomes "aaaahhhhh." I think of this saturation process as ZAPPING, because it reminds me of the movies where people get zapped or eliminated when they are no longer needed. Here you'll be zapping those "uh-oh" sections with the positive forces of breathing and sensory awareness to transform them into performer-friendly spots.

WHY DIDN'T I STUDY THE KAZOO?

The following steps are provided for you in your practice of such challenging moments. The Coda of Chopin's Fourth Ballade is used to demonstrate how to "zap" such moments. This is one of the piano literature's pinnacle pieces so please don't assume that "zapping" it is all that is needed to be able to play it. It is used to show that even with the toughest passage it is possible to change a mind-set. Combined with ease in playing, patience, quality practice and magic numbering (which goes up by a factor of 26,573 for a piece like this), there is a chance to make breakthroughs in even the toughest spots. (Your sense of humor should sit on your shoulder as well.)

(See music.)

As a preparatory exercise, take a few minutes away from the keyboard. The following exercise is intended to remind you of the feeling of staying with each moment at your instrument—or wherever you happen to be—in a relaxed

Chopin, Ballade in F Minor, Coda

manner, without giving your mind room for anticipating the next step. Recall that it is in those sometimes imperceptible anticipatory moments that tension loves to lodge.

Away from your instrument

You are going to walk across the room, one step at a time, by taking a step forward on one foot, then bringing your other foot together. You then:

1. Stop and cue into R/A as you stand in place. As you focus on breathing to the point of light, you fully ground yourself in your breathing. Feel the weight released into your arms, feet securely planted on the ground, spine extended into the floor behind you. When you are fully grounded in your breathing and standing solidly over your feet, take another step forward.

2. STOP and repeat the process.

    This deceptively simple exercise can have surprising results, which Leon was to discover.

    Leon came to see me because he was dissatisfied with his last performance. We had worked together before and he had impressively conquered his fear of playing for large audiences. I tried tracing where he had gotten derailed in this particular instance. When we reviewed the sequence of events that led to his accepting the invitation to play, he pinpointed a moment in time when he had the thought that this was not the right situation for him to perform. He had, however, talked himself out of his thoughts as being silly and leftover from his old frightened days. But the queasiness remained, and resulted in his unhappiness with the entire experience.

    I asked Leon to do the walking exercise, and wait before taking a step until he was fully aligned with his breathing, calming light, body, floor. He became most serious and took time after each step.

    Leon reported afterward that, as he took time checking in with himself before each step, he gained a sense of what it meant to be in tune with himself, true to himself. And that he probably wouldn't be able, even if he tried, to ignore his internal voice next time it wanted airspace.

When you finish crossing the room in this way, come back to your instrument.

At the keyboard

Sit at the piano with the music in front of you. It is crucial to have the Puppy Dog and Magic Carpet techniques mastered, so you might want to review them. (See chapter *Magic Carpet, Puppy Dog.*). Remember that for now the most important part of this exercise takes place *between*, not during the actual playing.

1. With hands lying in Puppy Dog in your lap, let the Magic Carpet bring your arms up to the keyboard.

    Begin playing the chords that immediately precede the coda. Stop after the last one.

2. Bring hands back into your lap. Cue into R/A. Keep awareness on your breathing until you are completely at ease.

    Take your time. Feel the calmness permeating your body.

    Look at the spot in the music and say something out loud such as: "This is easy," or, "I love this part. I can play it with ease." Use any phrase that brings you in touch with the beauty of the music and your own love of it.

3. Magic Carpet your hands back onto the keyboard and play a small part of the coda: one note, a half-bar, or a bar + the next down beat.

    Then hands back in lap, cue to R/A and repeat your phrase: " I love this part. I can play it."

    Wait until you are focused on your breathing, arms heavy. Take your time.

4. Play several bars this way, always arriving on a down beat.

5. Now go through the same process but when you stop at a down beat keep your hands over the notes instead of putting them in your lap. You focus on your breathing, get grounded and repeat out loud, "I love this part. I can play it."

6. Take a pencil and write your phrase on the music itself. You are visually reinforcing your practice of this hitherto problematic passage in two ways: by seeing the phrase written next to the passage on the music, and in seeing your Puppy Dog hands move easily as they play the passage. All this is done in a relaxed body state.

    You are re-training your body's kinesthetic response by replacing the former "uh-oh" response with calm. Once this is accomplished you are free to fill the relaxed response with musical expression, with passion. But it is important to fully reinforce the relaxed response in order not to relapse later on.

Therefore, in the next steps make sure you go slowly enough to keep track of your sensory system.

7. Start putting larger sections together now, 2, 4 or 8 bars at a time.

    Maintain ease of *arms/hands* (the Puppy Dog feel), *body* (grounded, relaxed), *mind* (thoughts of ease and loving the music). If you experience any interference, cue yourself immediately into R/A while continuing to play. If that is not possible, then stop playing and cue.

8. Increase the section you work on until you play the entire coda with ease.

9. Your final goal is of course playing the coda through at speed with ease. You can choose how to gain speed, but here are two ideas:

    • At the desired speed, go through steps from 4 to 7. Or,

    • Go directly to playing through the coda at speed, cueing yourself whenever necessary.

If the body needs more reinforcement to maintain its ease, you might decide to attain speed gradually rather than immediately.

It can't be repeated enough: you are training your body to relax in what has been a tension-provoking situation. This takes patience on your part. How many years has it taken your body to respond in the first way? Don't expect it to suddenly jump up and say: "Eureka. I've got it. I'll never get tense again." If you've ever trained a dog, you'll understand.

The dog, contrary to our desire, does not speak English. Neither do your hands. You, the trainer, must repeat a command some incredible magic number of times: *Sit.* **Reward, reward. Then,**

MAKING THE RELAXED/ALERT RESPONSE AUTOMATIC FOR THOSE "UH-OH" SPOTS more magic numbering of: *Sit*. Reward, reward. All this without venting anger or frustration. What gets the dog trained? Patience, persistence, calm and playfulness. And love. Why give yourself anything less?

And finally, you will discover by practicing this way, focusing first on breathing, then on sensory information, there isn't much space left for questioning thoughts or doubts to reside.

The question of maintaining ease in your hands and arms while feeling the internal intensity of musical emotion needs to be addressed. When musicians lose themselves in their music, they often experience the emotion throughout their body. This emotional intensity can translate into holding tension in hands or fingers. Here, you are training yourself to both feel your music intensely and keep hands/arms easy and relaxed. That is why it is important to be aware of and practice into the music, the emotional affect experienced internally, with the Puppy Dog, Magic Carpet ease experienced externally.

CHAPTER 7.

Deep Relaxation/Visualization: Working While Resting

No discussion of performance practice can neglect the value of deep relaxation/visualization as a practice tool. This entails getting into a deeply relaxed state, lying down, eyes closed, and rehearsing your performance by internally visualizing it. It is a confidence-building tool long known to athletes and artistic performers. In addition to being useful in preparing for performing, deep relaxation exercise can also unlock creative blocks. Sergei Rachmaninoff, at one time suffering from composer's block, was put once again in touch with his great powers through hypnosis, one of the deeper levels of this technique.

Deep Relaxation is different from the kind of relaxing with which you are familiar in the R/A state. The latter provides you with the means of remaining very alert though calm, aware of and connected to your environment. It is a pivotal state of mind/body that allows you to direct your attention where you wish, whether it remains on your breathing or directed to a sensory channel, and to achieve the action required, such as learning, memorizing or performing. In the deep relaxation exercise, you are entirely engaged in the exercise itself, in an altered state of mind. The body becomes totally relaxed; you are disengaged from your environment and focused entirely inward. Afterwards, you will surely find yourself in an utterly relaxed state, one that is not conducive to immediate activity.

For this reason, it is important that you practice deep relaxation/visualization only when you have enough time, both to get to that level of relaxation and afterward to gently and gradually re-enter your normal activity level. However, do practice this visualization often as a powerful adjunct to successful music-making, whether or not you perform. Eventually, you will apply it to many other areas of your life.

At the beginning, it is advisable to practice twice a day, for example in the morning and in the evening, for a minimum of 20 minutes each time.

After you first read this entire chapter, and before beginning the exercise, if there is any reason you feel uncomfortable about doing it, postpone it until consulting with someone you trust who practices visualization techniques or knows about them. If you have low blood pressure, consult your medical advisor. These exercises are done throughout the world, millions of relaxation tapes and self-hypnosis books are sold, and deep relaxation techniques are taught in many different kinds of classes, including stress management. So they are known to have beneficial effects. However, if this is your first time, or you don't know much about it, and have the slightest doubt about doing it by yourself, then just read this chapter now, and make more inquiries before proceeding on your own.

Turning to the visualization, I suggest you do one of the following before trying the exercise: if you do the visualization by yourself, then before lying down, familiarize yourself with the following suggestions by reading them over several times, or record the suggestions onto a tape, speaking slowly and giving yourself plenty of time to get relaxed. Then play it for yourself after getting in a comfortable position. Alternatively, you can have a friend lead you through by reading out loud, slowly, in a gentle tone of voice.

If you do this alone, you will say the phrases as they are written with the "I" pronoun, as for example, "I am feeling peaceful and calm." If a friend reads this to you, she will naturally substitute "You" for "I."

Deep Relaxation Visualization: At-One-With-the-Universe

1. Find a quiet place where you can lie down comfortably, shoes off, no tight clothing, with whatever pillows or blankets you might need.

   Pull the shades down if there's too much light.

   Take a few moments to shift around until you feel settled.

2. Take a big, big breath and exhale. Wait a moment, and take another long, deep breath and whoosh it out of you noisily.

   Take your time.

   Keep your eyes open until they eventually close by themselves.

3. Bring awareness to your breathing, as you breathe naturally in and out, with a slightly open mouth, an easy jaw.

   Enjoy the feeling of your body becoming more peaceful and more relaxed.

4. Start at the top of your head and work slowly down through every part of your body to your toes. Let the relaxation power enter and imagine it gently massaging every pore it touches as you say the following phrase:

VISUALIZING YOUR PERFORMANCE

   "And now I feel the relaxation power entering (part of body), and I feel more and more peaceful, more and more relaxed."

5. Start with your head and continue with:

   scalp, hair, forehead, eyebrows, eyes and all the tiny muscles around them, nose, cheeks, mouth, tongue, teeth, chin;

   down from your chin to throat, shoulders, arms, elbows, forearms, wrist, fingers;

   through your trachea, your lungs, and throughout your rib cage; your heart, diaphragm, lower abdomen;

   into the pelvic area, your buttocks, down into your thighs, knees, calves, shins, ankles, feet, toes.

6. Now, slowly count from 1 to 10, deepening your relaxed state, and letting your mind and body reach its own level of receptivity to effective practice or rehearsal.

   Slowly and gently say: "One… down…" "Two …down"….until you are at "Ten…completely peaceful, completely relaxed."

   You are at the perfect place now to do the work you set out to do.

7. Picture yourself in a setting that brings you peace and joy, a setting in which you are completely at ease with yourself… It may be at the beach… lying by the fireplace… engaged in an activity you love… alone… or with people.

See yourself in this situation…looking free…serene…happy…

Now let yourself *feel* that scene as if it were occurring this very moment…. For example, if at the beach, feel the warmth of the sun on your body…the softness of the sand under you…the ease and relaxation…*Smell* the air as you breathe…*hear* the sounds of the waves…. *See* the light play on the water…

Let the entirety of the scene permeate your being until you feel completely at one-with-the-universe…

Now, let your body come up with a cue, a symbol of this entire feeling-state…. The cue can be kinesthetic, a feeling inside you… visual…auditory…anything at all that conjures up this mind/body state for you…the feeling of ease and comfort in the world. This set of feelings will now be available to you anytime you wish to re-capture them by bringing up your symbol.

8. Remaining in this state of at-one-with-the-universe, you are going to gently change the scene—only the scene—not the feeling. The new scene is the site of your performance. It is right before you are to play. Watch yourself enter this new scene. Notice how you look, what you are wearing.

    Give yourself your at-one-with-the-universe cue…watch yourself walk on stage… notice your buoyancy… the feeling of belonging there…totally natural…totally at ease…savor the moment…. Watch as you go through your entire performance (in this altered state, you can condense time so it takes only a few minutes, or if you prefer, you can go through the entire performance in actual performing time, enjoying each piece from beginning to end)…

    You are aware of the surroundings as a holding environment…like air which provides you sustenance…alive, animated…connected in a mutual partnership…as you go through your performance you are keenly focused, animated, effortlessly in control yet feeling as if the music is being played through you…

    Let your feelings become words, words such as "pleasure"…"joy"…"effortless"…any words meaningful for you in this sublime experience…enjoy these moments…bask in the feeling…. Then slowly bring the performance to its natural end, and prepare yourself to return to the room you are in.

9. Slowly count yourself back from "ten" to "one" increasing your voice from gentle to more firm, more natural, as with the following suggestions:

    "*Ten*"—preparing to come back to normal state-of-mind

    "*Nine*"—beginning to feel the couch under me, and beginning to be aware of the sounds in the room…

"Eight"—(your voice sounding increasingly resonant and firm) beginning to feel the blood returning to normal circulation...starting to breathe more normally...

"Seven"—hearing more of the sounds in the room and outside...feeling more alive throughout my body...

"Six"—feeling more and more energized...

"Five"—half-way back...feeling sensations throughout my body...thinking about the rest of the day (or evening...)

"Four"—looking forward to continuing my activities...alert and rested...

"Three"—almost back to normal-day reality...my body alert...feeling rested...invigorated...looking forward to doing what I need to do...

"Two"—almost back...hearing all the sounds around me...breathing normally...

And *"One"*—(said in a completely normal tone of voice)—back to everyday reality...take a big breath and stretch...move feet...and, open eyes...

10. Slowly bring yourself to an upright position. Take a few moments to transition from the relaxed state to the more normal one. Do not jump back immediately into activity before gauging exactly how you feel.

This technique is a means of programming feelings of mastery and enjoyment into your body so that there is as seamless a transition as possible between pre-performing and actual performing. It can be used both to watch yourself perform, as you just did, or to go through actual physical practicing. Your muscles learn kinesthetically when you visualize practicing, thus making visualization an important adjunctive tool for performers.

Deep relaxation/visualization should be practiced regularly (surprise, surprise), but reserved for those times when you can take the time to let your body come back to its natural level of energy afterwards. It is one technique among many at your disposal in the integrated process of performing. In my experience it should not be used too close in time to the actual performance because of its potential enervating effect on the body.

You probably already incorporate visualization into your life, whether it's picturing what's in your refrigerator when shopping without a list, or mentally picturing your wardrobe while imagining what outfit you'll put together for that special event.

In the novel *Memoirs of a Geisha,* the apprentice geisha Sayuri, must learn to play the shamisen, a Japanese stringed instrument, and to dance elegantly. Here she describes her own visualization techniques.

> I began to discover little tricks that made everything go more smoothly. For example, I found a way of practicing the shamisen while running errands. I did this by practicing a song in my mind while picturing clearly how my left hand should shift on the neck and how the plectrum should strike the string. In this way, when I put the real instrument onto my lap, I could sometimes play a song quite well even though I had tried playing it only once before. Some people thought I'd learned it without practicing, but in fact, I'd practiced it all up and down the alleyways of Gion…I used a different trick to learn the…other songs…I took to writing the words on a piece of paper before going to sleep. Then when I awoke, while my mind was still soft and impressionable, I read the page before even stirring…with music…I used a trick of finding images to remind me of the tune. For example, a branch falling from a tree might make me think of the sound of a drum, or a stream flowing over a rock might remind me of bending a string on the shamisen to make the note rise in pitch; and I would picture the song as a kind of stroll through a landscape.

There are stories about the legendary pianists Josef Hoffman and Josef Lhevinne, who learned new pieces en route by train to give their next concert. One can only imagine what powers of visualization these giants of the piano must have had.

And the brilliant British actress Susan Hampshire, featured in several lengthy series on Masterpiece Theatre, where her many roles entailed learning thousands and thousands of pages of script, writes of the crippling dyslexia from which she suffers. Describing reading as "a torture," she devised an elaborate system of colors, signs and lines superimposed on the script to help her recognize the meaning of a sentence, or pick out a word. While learning to drive a car she used another device, now hopefully familiar to you, dear reader: she repeated out loud every instruction her teacher gave her. For Susan Hampshire, laboring under extreme disadvantage, such measures were mandatory, making the difference between succeeding and failing.

Imagine what a difference harnessing such measures can make under more normal circumstances.

CHAPTER 8.

Where's the Expression?

There is a different breath in every breather.
William Saroyan

You have been laying the foundation for solid learning, memorizing and per-forming. It entails the conscious application of principles, detailed work, and lots of practice. What happens to spontaneity? If you practice everything, what room is left to endow the music with the immediacy of feeling at the moment of performance? The last thing you want is for your music to sound like a tech-nical exercise. And building in the passion, delineating how every single note must be played, every nuance programmed, can sound stilted or impersonally expressive. I call such playing "mannered musicality"—music properly shaped and nuanced, but leaving little room for spontaneous individual expression. Play "from the inside out," was how Margaret Rowell, great cello teacher, cajoled her students into infusing their music with passion.

You *can* play accurately, musically *and* passionately. Knowing how to prac-tice well gives you the secure foundations from which to soar. Wang Fang-yu, great calligrapher of the twentieth century, said that discipline frees the hand to do as the heart and mind bid. Such was actor John Gielgud's mastery of his art and security in his role, that he once declared in an interview that he might mentally go over his shopping list while on stage. Such is the mastery for which you have been preparing.

But while attaining mastery it is important to remember the ultimate goal. Such security should be like the trunk of a tree: connected to firm foundation in order to free the branches to improvise movement, bend, arch and stretch according to the dictates of its ever-changing environment.

Like an actor, and a tree, your entire body is your medium. And like them, you need to have a pliant, limber body so that the music, like the actor's character, flows out easily, in a supple, unlabored, natural fashion. Up to now you have been using preparation techniques designed to tame and direct your energy. You must also know techniques to release and free your energy. It is to those we now turn.

Movement into Music

There is an additional *pre-sitting-down* element that is an invaluable adjunct to your preparation repertoire: that of stretching and moving, whether slow and graceful, like tai chi, or more vigorous, like running, skipping and jumping. It can be any series of motions that limber your body, expend excess energy, or contain and mobilize your energy. One of my fondest performance memories is running along the beach with my four-hand piano partner Elizabeth before performing at a site near-by. We laughed at the ludicrousness of it, and the sheer pleasure of running under the stars in the sand, as we belted out some rhythmic interludes exchanged between our parts. When we came back to change clothing and settle down, we were red-cheeked, hearts pounding. But we experienced that pounding as exhilaration, not anxiety, and that exhilaration infused our playing which soared to new heights that night.

Actors, like dancers, have routines of body exercise, from limbering the mouth and voice to whole-body movements. They do wonderfully crazy-looking exercises such as playing out different emotions using a single sound. For example, using only the "ah" sound, they play out fear, anger, sadness, seduction. All this frees them from internal restrictions on self-expression.

Since you also are a performer whose instrument is your whole body, an active, physical and hopefully playful kind of exercise should always be utilized in conjunction with your practice. Make up your own series of movements to precede practicing, just as the dancer does her warm-ups. Then, immediately before performing, for example when waiting backstage, limber up with movements that free you and expend excess energy. Experiment with just how much pre-playing expenditure of energy helps prepare your body; too much will enervate you, but the right amount will not only relax you but dissipate anxious energy that might otherwise interfere with playing.

Drama into Music

Once your body is pliant and supple, it is more free to give expression to the musical character of each piece. And every piece, like every character on stage, has its own essence: Chopin's "Prelude in E Minor" will always have the quality of yearning, let us say, just as Hamlet will always be tortured by his conflicting emotions. As each actor imbues "Hamlet" with complex qualities from within himself, you, a complex person in your own right, imbue the "Prelude" with your own quality of yearning. The practice techniques help free you to express *your version* of that yearning, not imitate someone else's.

> "Put your own feeling into the music which you are playing. Even if it is not always the right one, I would rather have that than none at all or merely what you have been taught," admonished Clara Schumann, in a letter to her daughter, Eugenie.

How do all these techniques come together to free the performer in you to be both character-actor and self-expressive? The answer is, in surprisingly similar ways to those employed by the actor and dancer.

Look at the opening of Bach's "French Ouverture in B Minor." A deliberate B minor chord in the bass sets the scene for the stately suite that follows. You approach this piece with some knowledge of French style, its sweep, grandeur, courtly gesture, and with the sound of the chord, rolled upward where it is suspended in air for a moment before being joined with a flourish in the upper voice. You let yourself "become the statue" that *is* the opening chord for you: perhaps with body straight, hands and arms thrust outward and slightly upward in a regal gesture. You go to the piano as the chord-statue and find yourself with back erect, head held high. You throw down the chord, this time playing not from the solar plexus but from the straightening of the back

With this opening statue-gesture epitomizing the over-all character of the music, you set the scene for the music to unfold. Practicing based on breathing, sensory perception, and the full body kinesthetic response, prepares you not only to become a vessel for Bach's music, but to become a passionate one as well.

We can summarize the steps that occur like this:

In a moment of time, you breathe easily into your body, creating its state of receptivity. Simultaneously, you hear the music internally, then as it sets off vibrations in your inner ear. Through the connections made by your breathing and ability to direct sensory perception, the music thus heard is directed to all the kinesthetic places in your body, all the places in which feeling resides, setting up waves between them. The body is activated to move internally if imperceptibly with those musical waves. You perceive

77

the music physically, as it moves through the body, inducing its own natural laws of internal movement.

Your expression lies embedded in your feelings, which are the kinesthetic responses. Thus, by connecting to your kinesthetic senses, you are connecting to the repository of your unique experience, which constitutes your essential self. At its most free, the expression that emanates is a result of the totality of your life experiences to date, both successes and failures. Why the failures as well? Because if you only play from your positive being you deprive the music of the rest of what makes you human. Once we start filtering aspects of our personality, we prohibit that energy from informing the music, depriving the music of the complexity it deserves.

Part of enlarging your experience as a performer involves, like an actor, delving into the character and history of the music you play. "I have not got a character until I have mastered exactly how he walks...know his mind...find out how he thinks, how he feels, his background, his mannerisms," Sir Alec Guinness remarked upon preparing to play roles as varied as Obi-Wan Kenobi and Hamlet. Likewise, Brenda Blethyn, playing a working-class woman of the 1970's in "Secrets and Lies," studied "Help Wanted" ads in the newspapers of that time to see what jobs would be available to her character, and how they would curtail the options she'd have in life.

The pianist seeking the character, the gesture, the statue for Bach's "French Ouverture" will necessarily be familiar not only with Bach's style, but the French Ouverture style as well, and its historical framework. Thus, your personal expression comes from the totality of your personal experience conjoined to your understanding of your art. In this way, the statue and ensuing movement, which is your interpretation, is completely individual at the same time it taps into universal roots.

You can play with the concepts of statues and motion in mental as well as physical practice. In conceiving of the gesture that defines musical character, you as actor can imbue that gesture or statue with a life or a dance of its own, letting it lead you directly into the fuller movement of the music. The statue is like a painting that starts out as an outline on the canvas, and then gets filled with design, motion and color. In other words, the gesture, which is static, is both an intense body experience as well as the jumping-off point to further character development of the music and to the discovery of its passion.

Teachers often use colorful, descriptive narrative in eliciting expression from students. "Twinkle like the first evening star." "Hiss like a cornered cat." "Growl." Here you are taking the next step by actually *becoming* the first evening star, the cornered cat, the growl.

Stanislavski tells actors-to-be that: …"*a real artist must lead a full, interesting, beautiful, varied, exacting and inspiring life.*"

And so it is for the musician. In order to be expressive you must have something to express. In order to fulfill your complexity as a human being, you must open yourself to life. As we discuss in the Coda, the pianist is both artistic and creative. Through the exercises in this guide you have garnered the preparatory tools to become a creative personality at the keyboard, as in life. In becoming an expressive, passionate and complex person, you reach for artistic realms as well.

The artist struggles to achieve the highest levels of self-expression, expression that moves others because it is universal in essence. The young protagonist seeking gold in *The Illustrated Alchemist* comes to an understanding about intuition as a "sudden immersion of the soul into the universal current of life, where the histories of all people are connected…" I think that applies equally to artistic expression. It is the individual speaking a universal language through her own, individual voice.

Part III

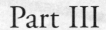

PERFORMING

Breathe in experience, breathe out poetry.

Muriel Rukeyser, poet

CHAPTER 9.

Crossing-Over From Practice to Performing: The Practice Performance

You are now at the cross-over moment from practicing to performing.

You have at your disposal the means to control the state of your mind/body response and the means of focusing awareness onto any number of sensory focal points. Your goal is to play in a state of integration between yourself, your instrument, the music and your environment. Over time, your self-conscious practice lays the foundation for crossing-over into a seamless un-self-consciousness.

All this takes practice, good practice, repeated practice: quality joined with quantity. All this is so the actual performance can be like no other time you've played because you will be as free as possible to *be* with the music and the moment, and to animate and connect yourself to that unique moment.

It is analogous to building your dream-house: those hours and hours (sometimes years) of conscious decision-making, planning, laying of foundation, choosing materials, considering options and choices, room designs, construction techniques. The moment comes when all the work is over and you actually move into your home, walk through the rooms, live the life for which you have created a home base. Likewise, your performing can be like moving in to inhabit your musical being. And before the actual house warming, or performance, you must prepare room by room, step by step to make sure you have everything you need.

Your first step is to go through an entire performance in your home, testing yourself with some amount of distraction. Your goal is to play the whole program exactly as you wish to perform it, undisturbed by any external or internal distractions which might arise.

I suggest you wear the same performing outfit and play at the same time of day as your actual performance. No matter that it feels strange putting on your long black taffeta gown with the spaghetti straps at two in the afternoon to play in the toy-strewn living room. This is the time to discover that the gown makes swooshing noises as you move on the bench, or the straps are

PRE-PERFORMANCE PRACTICE RUN-THROUGH IN YOUR LIVING ROOM

allergic to your shoulders and keep escaping; or those fashionably high heels elevate your feet to a ridiculous angle from the floor, putting creases at your ankles that don't belong.

At one of my adult student workshops Deborah, a normally well-prepared woman, had a surprisingly hard time concentrating. Her playing didn't go well, and she was puzzled. After everyone played, they discussed the evening's performances. Suddenly Deborah declared: "I got it. I always practice in the morning after I dress but with my slippers still on. It felt so different wearing my regular work shoes, with the heels. It totally threw me!"

Likewise, since light is different at different times of day, and you feel different in the morning, afternoon and evening, it's important to do this run-through at the same time as the scheduled performance if that is at all possible. These are some areas of the performing process to take into consideration as you begin to prepare. We'll cover others in the next chapter "The Performance Schedule."

Right now you're starting to think in terms of making your performance as rich a sensory experience for you and your audience as that with which you endowed your practicing. Being comfortable, looking good—all are part of the performing process.

For the cross-over exercise you can choose between two possible avenues. The first is to enlist a friend to be present, listening but also distracting. She can walk around, hum, make phone calls, even talk to you. She should also listen in silence for long periods of time, allowing you to experience what it's like when your audience completely focuses on you. Throughout all this your job is to keep focused, and to play your entire recital.

Another approach is to close off the room in which you play and alert others in the house to what you are doing, that is, going through your performance and that you are therefore unavailable. But don't tell them to keep things quiet. Don't take the phone off the hook (you just won't be available to talk). They can even come in and let you know someone's on the phone for you. But you continue playing as if nothing were happening; you ignore your nosy older sister speaking on the phone to your boyfriend or your baby brother playing space cowboys under the piano.

HERE ARE THE GUIDELINES FOR THIS PRACTICE PERFORMANCE:

1. Set up your tape recorder.

2. Decide how you will officially enter the performing arena. Then, before entering, do your limbering exercises and/or R/A to get into the mind/body state you desire.

3. Once you begin a piece, you must finish it exactly as you would in performance no matter what happens. No starting and stopping.

4. If you get distracted, immediately bring your awareness onto breathing straight to your Calming Light while continuing to play.

5. Immediately after the performance, take inventory of what methods worked for you, and which need more practice. If there were memory slips, take out those sections and *zap* them, using the Eight-Point Sensory System.

6. If you had moments when your mind was not at ease despite the fact you were able to play accurately, practice the "breathing—stop—this is easy" exercise, until, "This is easy. I love this part" (or your equivalent statement) replaces the thoughts previously making your mind uneasy.

7. Listen to the recording and honestly evaluate not only the spots that need attention, but also all the beautiful moments you brought to the music.

If you practice this way, are you guaranteed perfection? No more than you are guaranteed a perfect home once it is built. But by paying attention to the details as well as the over-all architecture, by not leaving to fate what it is possible for you to control, you pave the way for falling in love with the finished house, as with your finished performance. It is like Arthur Rubinstein once said, here paraphrased: "If you practice 100 percent you will play 75 percent." Therefore, you must practice 200 percent. That means using all available resources within yourself—mental, physical, emotional, rational, and irrational—and that is what you are learning to do.

CHAPTER 10.

The Performance Schedule

Itzhak Perlman told the story years ago about getting ready for his Carnegie Hall debut. In essence, this is what he did. Setting a date for himself a good three months ahead of the real concert, he prepared for the fictitious date as if it were the actual Carnegie Hall debut. For a period of time previous to this self-appointed date, he enforced his own style of discipline concerning activities. In other words, he completely geared up for his big concert three months early.

On the night of his self-appointed "debut" he dressed in concert garb. He waited in the "wings" of the stage, the kitchen of his apartment, and at the appointed hour he stepped out onto the "stage," his very own living room. He presented his debut. There was no audience. He took his bows, came back-stage to the kitchen at intermission and at the conclusion of his concert took his final bows. (Undoubtedly, he imagined thunderous applause.)

Perlman declared he was every bit as nervous that evening as he imagined he would be at his debut. Three months later he was able to enjoy his own debut.

What can we learn from Perlman's experience?

To begin with, you must schedule pre-performance performances. They should be in circumstances as closely resembling the actual performing circumstances as possible. In *Into Thin Air*, the thrilling account of a failed Mt. Everest climb, Jon Krakauer writes of the importance of practicing on increasingly difficult expeditions, not on little hills, before climbing a major mountain. There is no substitute for partaking in the real event. Naturally, it isn't always possible to give a run-through at the actual site. But there should be a minimum of three run-throughs after your cross-over performance at home, and once again they should be in the same attire and same hour of day as the performance.

The importance of rehearsing in the same attire bears emphasis. Not only do you want to find out whether those pants zip up properly, or whether the sleeves on that dress droop onto the keyboard, competing with your fingers for airspace. You also want to be familiar with the actual *experience of dressing* for your performance. Perhaps, if you've given your rehearsal performances in those beloved tattered jeans, and on the day of your actual performance you reach to pull out your concert garb from its plastic wrap at the back of your closet, you might experience something like I did years ago.

While preparing for a recital, I looked forward to the moment right before performing, when I'd put on my beautiful purple velvet skirt and it would transform me into a fairy princess. I'd never worn the skirt while playing, but I'd worn it to many parties and always felt beautiful in it. I reached for it that day. Suddenly my body discovered a whole new set of sensations as my mind ceaselessly whirred. Had there been words to the whirring, it might have been these:

"Ohmygod. This is it."

(The rational mind tries to rationalize): "Hey, it's just like going to a party. Soon you'll be a fairy princess."

"Ohmygod. This is it."

"Hey, remember—you're completely prepared to play. What's this all about?"

"Ohmygod. This is it."

"You're repeating yourself."

"Ohmygod…"

I'm not suggesting you won't have pre-performance dialogues or jitters anyway. Only that you want to minimize the possibility of being caught off guard. It's worth a few extra cleaning bills to incorporate your attire into the performance ritual.

You should also practice the non-musical aspects such as what you will eat and drink, and how late you will stay up the night before, as part of the preparatory process. Find out what foods agree with you the day of your performance by experimenting on the days of your pre-performance run-throughs. *Don't* experiment on the day of your actual performance. (A banana, by the way, is a wonderful snack, easy on the stomach and rich in potassium.) The bottom line is: take charge of the things over which you have control. For the rest, use techniques like the ones in this book to create the optimum mental preparation for responding to whatever happens, as in the 'at-one-with-the-universe' exercise.

A good friend of mine is a dog trainer, and we've worked together to alleviate her performance anxiety when showing and competing in dog shows. She related the following delicious incident. She had thoroughly prepared herself mentally for an important show, gone through many practices with her dogs, and had finally gotten to the point of looking forward to what had once been an unnerving experience. Confident that nothing was going to deflect her concentration, she did not reckon with the sprinkler system going on in the middle of her dog's routine, wreaking havoc with the *dog's* concentration. So much for all her preparatory work. Perhaps moments like these occur to remind us to keep our sense of humor and perspective, and to realize there are situations we cannot foresee nor control. My friend did, however, subsequently incorporate the sprinkler system in practice with her dogs.

Which brings us to the issue of practicing your recital at the actual site of performance. If the site is available you should naturally avail yourself of this golden opportunity. After making sure the sprinkler system isn't activated by any of your repertoire, here are some suggestions on how to use that time.

If you are a pianist you naturally test the piano with parts or all of the program. Bring along a tape recorder and a friend who gives you honest feedback. The tape and your friend will each give you different perspectives. Remember the sound will be different when there are people in the hall. But in addition to playing, you can use some of the approaches already practiced in making the whole music-making process friendlier and more fulfilling. In the same way you explored and made your instrument your partner, you can make the *environment of your performance* a partner as well.

Walk around the room or recital hall using the same sensory awareness you developed at your instrument by opening up your audio, visual and kinesthetic channels. *Listen* to the hall, both standing still with eyes closed, and when walking around. Take in the *visual* aspects, enjoying the variety of textures and colors. *Touch* the walls, chairs, stage curtains remembering: *a mind free to respond connects and animates.* By connecting with and animating the space you create an intimate, personal relationship of integrated unity between yourself and your environment, the very feeling you created for yourself in your 'at-one-with-the-universe' visualization, and in your partnership with your instrument.

Now walk around the seats, sitting down in different parts of the room. Become your own audience for a moment, watching and listening to the imaginary you on stage. What is your 'gut' reaction as you watch yourself walk out on stage and begin to play? What thoughts do you send to yourself up there? Who do you imagine sitting in various chairs at the recital?

Arkady, a fine pianist, was surprised at the anxiety he was feeling the afternoon of his evening performance. We spent some time together in a mock performance situation. Here is what I remember happening at our session, followed by his own recollections.

> **Arkady** was nervous about who might be in the audience. So I role-played what I thought could be the worst-case scenario. Imagining ourselves at that evening's recital, Arkady walked out on stage, noticed me in the audience, then came over and asked how I came to be there. I answered in my best tough-guy voice: "Me? I got dragged here by my wife. I dunno anything about this here classical music. Give me my choice, I'd be home watching the game on TV." Taken aback, Arkady stood there a moment. I was wondering whether his first impulse was to give this obnoxious imaginary character a sock in the jaw, (and hoped he remembered it was really just his good friend). But suddenly he took on the challenge. "Well, sir I'm really pleased you came anyway, and I'm going to play just for you to show that you can enjoy music as well as baseball."
>
> Arkady remembers talking to members of the audience. "Telling them about why I was doing the program and what I was afraid of seemed to demystify the aura surrounding the audience for me. Also, dancing the movement of the sonata that felt blocked was really helpful. It kept me in my body and out of my head when I played that night."

That evening I heard Arkady play with more than his usual élan. He later confided that he was particularly motivated to move the reluctant baseball fan with his playing.

PERFORMANCE SCHEDULE AT A GLANCE

1. Aim to be at performance level by a date well ahead of the actual performance.

2. Give at least three performances before this date, approximating as closely as possible the actual performance situation. Things to consider are: site, clothing, time of day, food (eat what you know will give you energy without filling you up), medications (if you plan on taking beta-blockers for anxiety, be sure to do so at your run-throughs to get used to their effect).

3. Tape record your performances and review areas that felt even slightly uneasy, using R/A, Eight-Point Sensory System and visualization.

4. Program into your schedule 'vacation' time for your pieces. They need time off, just like people. A good time to let pieces rest is when they are well prepared and you're feeling good about them. After their vacation, they come back refreshed and even more integrated.

And you, pianist, musician, performer—you have worked extremely well and now deserve to enjoy the fruits of your efforts. As you look back on the time it took you to get to this point in the slow, conscientious way necessary, think not only of what you accomplished as a musician but also how your efforts have changed the non-musical facets of your life. Without haste, take inventory of any changes, no matter how subtle, that have taken place since embarking on this process. When are you less frantic than before since practicing breathing to your internal light? Do you have less ache in some part of your body since relaxing shoulders and arms? Do you feel less overwhelmed by tasks now, approaching them a step at a time? Let your mind wander, stay attuned to your humor, and remain open for surprises.

Now the moment for your own performance approaches. In the time actors take to review their script and get into character before crossing-over into that sublime state, let's briefly review the entire integrated process.

CHAPTER 11.

Passionate Practice: A REVIEW

Here is a review of the techniques discussed for becoming a passionate musician.

Relaxing the Mind and Body

THE R/A EXERCISE

STEPS

- Awareness on your breathing to internal image, easy jaw
- Tension released from shoulders, arms heavy
- Easy arms and hands
- Magic Carpet lifts your arms and holds them up at the keyboard
- Fingers in Puppy Dog position

CUE

- You can use any element from this exercise to cue you into an easy frame of mind and body: the internal image, easy jaw, Puppy Dog fingers, heavy arms, Magic Carpet lifting and supporting arms

USES

- Anytime. During practice, while learning new pieces, while working on previously difficult spots. During performance, immediately upon distraction.

DIRECTING YOUR FOCUS

- The Eight-Point Sensory System
- Linking up sensory channels with each other, for example: linking the vibrations that the music sets off in your ears with the internal kinesthetic sensations and the sensation of fingers touching instrument.

INITIATING MUSICAL FLOW BEFORE AND DURING PERFORMANCE

THE STATUE

- Becoming the "statue" that embodies the feeling of the piece
- Letting the statue take on its own life and movement
- Breathing a connection from the "statue" to your internal kinesthetic sense, thereby tapping into your personal source of expression

CREATING PARTNERSHIP WITH THE INSTRUMENT

- Before performing on a new instrument, taking a moment to touch, connect and animate
- During practice as a regular exchange of feelings between the instrument and you

TAKING CARE OF JITTERS

PHYSICALLY

- Relatively hard exercise: running
- Light exercise: gentle moving, dance-like gestures

MENTALLY

- Long-term visualization
- R/A

PERFORMANCE DAY: ALREADY SCRIPTED

- Clothing, food, and activities

THE PERFORMANCE

- Using your own combination of sensory awareness, physical exercise and R/A to ground yourself
- Becoming-one-with-universe by establishing contact with place of performing, and through visualization
- While performing, when you experience interference: immediately cue to focusing on breathing, and away from playing. Since your body knows the piece so well, you will continue to play as if in an altered state during the few moments you need to ground yourself by breathing. Once grounded, you rejoin the music still in progress by focusing through the sensory channel(s) that most reliably bring you back.

CHAPTER 12.

Your Performance

You have put together many experiences in relation to making music. As you prepare to perform, it is time to set up your own ideal performing situation based on everything you have discovered.

The following pages are your Performance Checklist, yours to fill in. They are meant to serve as a guideline to help you perform optimally. You might begin by making copies of these pages so you can write in, check off, cross out, as you like for each performance.

Good Luck

PERFORMANCE CHECKLIST

1. PERFORMANCE SCHEDULE

Date of actual performance _____

Date to be at performance level _____

Date of cross-over performance at home _____

Dates of three run-throughs

1. _____

2. _____

3. _____

2. PRACTICE SCHEDULE

(include any vacation times from practice for yourself and for individual pieces)

Week (date)	Monday (times)	Tuesday	Wednesday	Thursday	Friday	Saturday	Sunday

3. VISUALIZATION PRACTICE SCHEDULE

Week (date)	Monday (times)	Tuesday	Wednesday	Thursday	Friday	Saturday	Sunday

4. Cueing to Breathing

• Note when you used it automatically during the day.

• Note the times you were able to breathe easily and maintain calm while having thoughts that previously would have upset you.

• Note the situations in which it would have been helpful had you cued to breathing.

5. Partnership With Your Instrument

Note the sense you have about your instrument as your partner.

6. Your Performance Outfit

(Be sure to wear it at all your run-throughs.)

7. Activities and Food for the Performing Day

(Be sure to note them at your first run-through, then evaluate and revise if necessary.)

8. Evaluation of Each Run-Through, Immediately Afterward

List everything that worked, everything that needs more work. Try the form on the following page.

Evaluation of Pre-Performance Run-Throughs

Run-Through #	1	2	3
Most successful areas			
Pre-performance preparation, mental & physical			
Sections needing work			
Clothing			
Food			
Activities of the day			

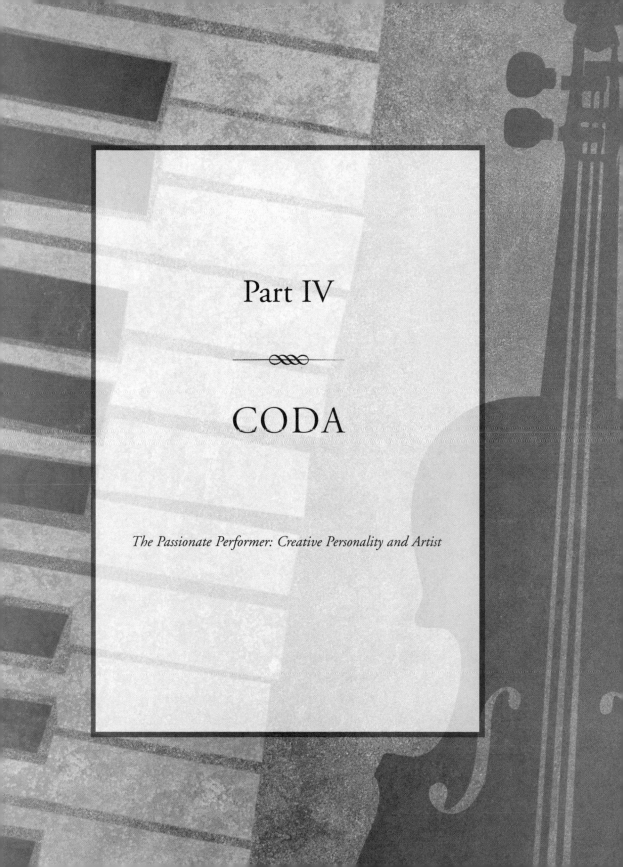

Part IV

CODA

The Passionate Performer: Creative Personality and Artist

CHAPTER 13.

The Passionate Performer

We are the sum of all the moments of our lives—
all that is ours is in them: we cannot escape or conceal it…

Thomas Wolfe

As you enter the performing arena you are confronted with the paradox of being a performer. Up to this moment, you have diligently prepared to make your playing as predictable and as easy as possible. You have been creative in your preparation and practice, drawing upon your mind, brain, body and your various modes of self-expression to elicit the fullest meaning from your music. To the extent that it is possible and desirable, you have also "normalized" performing by ironing out the edges between your regular life and your life as a musician. Much of this preparatory work entails grappling with and mastering the intent of the composer and of the music. Seen this way, performing is a re-creative art.

Yet, performing necessitates something more challenging from you, something quite out of the ordinary, sublime. It requires you to bring yourself, warts and all, to the music, to invest it with an individual meaning that is uniquely yours. And at the same time that you bring your entire being to the performing process, as Wolfe declares of the writer, you also surrender your very being to the process itself. In the paradoxical process of investing yourself in the music while surrendering to it, you cross-over into the realm of true artistry, for it is from that realm that something truly unique emerges.

You cross-over from the time of anticipation to that of participation: from anticipating as you consciously mold, ponder, work and refine; to that moment of letting-go, freeing your conscious self to participate in the totality of the musical experience—to becoming your instrument, becoming the music. You have mastered the experiential components of this cross-over in learning to breathe awareness through your sensory channels and into the music. But when that cross-over is spiritually as well as physically accomplished, you step from a known to an unknown reality, immortal and transcendent. This is how Cecilia Bartoli expresses the moment of participation:

...sometimes I am transported myself with the music, and perhaps that passes over to the audience. But there isn't a word for that. It's beautiful...Sometimes I feel that I am possessed, I don't know by what. Perhaps by God...It is as if I am separate from my body, I can look back and see myself from far away.

No wonder that anxiety often finds a comfortable niche, for that cross-over moment presents the ultimate challenge facing any performer, encapsulating as it does the entire artistic process. For the artist who engages in the artistic process is continually balancing opposites: hubris and humility, consciousness and unselfconsciousness, individuality and one's place in the larger commonality. Artists confront responsibility not only to themselves but also to their art, their community; performers confront as well their responsibility to composers. How then is it possible for a performer not to be anxious?

The Role of Anxiety

Anxiety, precisely because it is part of the process, must be confronted and incorporated as a catalyst rather than impediment. It is important not to sweep your fears under the carpet. It is important not to deny your most human flaws their place on the bench with you.

Here are two adult piano students grappling with their personal demons, demons born in that niche where anxiety resides.

> **Françoise**, a most talented piano student, was going through a practice performance at an evening workshop. She started playing then stopped, started and stopped over and over. I took her out to the hallway. "What's going on Françoise?"
>
> "I don't know. I wanted so badly to play tonight in front of the others and show off how much better I've gotten. But now I can't get into the music because I feel guilty about wanting to show off." She located the feeling holding her back in the pit of her stomach. "Go right to that feeling," I told her, "and let it become the performer. Give it free reign, Françoise. See what happens." Given the freedom to fully identify with what in fact she was feeling, her playing took on new life. Once she was able to give expression to such "unlofty" ideals, she could turn more freely to give full expression to the music.

Tom, another adult, was emotionally in knots about returning to music lessons. Every time he sat down he felt the spirit of his deceased father heavily pervading the atmosphere. His father had been severely judgmental as Tom grew up. Tom had learned well to internalize the critic. I asked Tom to imagine inviting his father to sit in on his lesson. With great trepidation he did so. When he played he felt the burning eyes bore into his back from the couch on which his father sat. "Talk to him," I encouraged. "Find out what your father is feeling as he hears you play." Tom engaged in a dialogue with the father in his imagination. He discovered his father had wanted desperately to play the piano himself but had not had the opportunity. His feelings while listening to Tom were a complex mixture of pride and jealousy tinged with sorrow and anger at his own sense of loss. His harsh criticism came from his own overriding need to deny the suffering that this sense of loss and deprivation caused. Tom, noticeably affected, softened. "Ask your dad to join you on the bench, and play for him directly." Apprehensive, Tom complied. He was crying as he played for his father. Slowly his internal experience of his father expanded to encompass the man's multidimensionality. With this expanded awareness of himself, Tom continued to study the piano.

"Energy is where the scary part is," declared Thomas Wolfe. To deny anxiety is to empower it. The same advice given to drivers never to turn the wheel in the opposite direction if the car veers out of control pertains here: go *right into the movement.*

Twelve year old Angela was part of a workshop I gave for the young participants of Junior Bach. She said she was "spooked out" when she thought about her impending audition. "Draw what 'spooked out' looks like," I said. She drew a page full of beautifully colored butterflies. "What are they trying to tell you?" She looked at the page, a broad smile soon overtaking her face. "They want to play with me at the audition." "Are you surprised?" She shook her head yes. "Would you like to let them?" She smiled yes again. She later told me they all played together and "I couldn't believe I had fun."

Angela's lesson for us: breathe directly to your "butterfly" area, watch them, and let yourself vibrate to their vibrations. Then notice—don't force—your body getting into sync with the sensation. Give your anxieties free rein to flutter so they aren't fluttering against confinement, and give yourself free rein to feel them. *Go right into the movement.*

At this point your own creativity can take over: you can name these anxieties, ("Yup, here's Hurricane Joe.") draw them, speak with them:

"What d'ya want now Joe?"

"Just checking in here."

"Well, if you check in, you gotta pull your weight. Start helping me practice." Working with your internal visitors transforms rather than constricts your own energy.

If you are lucky enough to experience a variety of nervous symptoms during your run-through performances, you have the golden opportunity of testing out a variety of responses. For example, if your foot starts shaking while you are playing, you can (in addition to the same techniques used with the butterflies):

- Exaggerate the shaking
- Start shaking the other foot
- Purposely practice for your next run-through by shaking your feet during practice
- _____(something you have discovered)

The important point is to keep yourself integrated, that is, feeling as a cohesive being, not in conflict between body and spirit but, even in a nervous state, at-one-with-yourself. That way you are more poised to make the cross-over into the realm for which there is no name.

The Performer as Creative Personality

Before we end this foray into the vast arena of integrated musicianship, it would be exciting to notice how the perspectives you have cultivated as students of music apply equally to the cultivation of the creative personality. The following are a few of the attributes that the performer and the creative person share.

A heightened sensory awareness. The Eight-Point Sensory System helped open all your sensory channels for the sake of good practicing. Creative people are, like artists, keenly alive to sensory perceptions, seeing what others often miss, receptive to non-verbal cues others dismiss. Feel the following description of color by Toni Morrison's character Pilate in *Song of Solomon:*

> *You think dark is just one color, but it ain't. There're five or six kinds of black. Some silky, some woolly. Some just empty. Some like fingers. And it don't stay*

still. It moves and changes from one kind of black to another. Saying something is pitch black is like saying something is green. What kind of green? Green like my bottles? Green like a grasshopper? Green like a cucumber, lettuce, or green like the sky is just before it breaks loose to storm? Well, night black is the same way. May as well be a rainbow.

Performers must likewise have a painter's palette of *tone-colors* in their repertoire to produce the full spectrum of human and spiritual experience.

In addition, when you have developed your own sensory awareness fully, you are less likely to be duped by others or by public opinion. You will know, for example, someone is lying despite his earnest look and sincere tone of voice, because your senses send you signals. Like Leon who became in "tune with himself" as he walked slowly across the room, you too have practiced paying attention to your sensory signals, kept an open line of communication to them and now trust them when they alert you not to trust this person, or enter that situation despite contrary advice. The creative personality you have cultivated will indeed alert you when the emperor has no clothes.

The ability to find useful commonality amongst disparate ideas. You have found commonality amongst the different art forms, using them to inform your own music-making power. Becoming a statue to uncover a musical character, giving voice to inner physical sensations in order to transform anxiety, drawing your instrument to create friendship—all these call upon your own creativity in the service of musical development.

Gehry, architect of the notable Guggenheim Museum in Bilbao, Spain reports that, in playing with forms for his structures he often finds them in strange places, like trash in wastepaper baskets, and in spaces between people.

A hunger for knowledge and a variety of experiences. We have already seen that Stanislavski advised actors-to-be to "lead a full, interesting, beautiful, varied, exacting and inspiring life." Musicians too need to continually expand their horizons. Read many kinds of books, travel, listen to a radio station you never heard before—do whatever you can to become a full, well-rounded individual. Then, not only does your music reflect your unique personality imbued with the vastness of your rich personal experience, but the relationships in the rest of your life will reflect these qualities as well.

The view that each experience has potential meaning. At the same time that the creative person seeks broadening experiences, he understands that everything that happens in his life adds to the fabric of his existence, deepening the personal source of knowledge from which the full, rich self emerges. Not every experience is of equal importance, but cumulatively they form the totality of personal integrity that then gets poured into the artist's creation or performance. Thus, the musician allows this cumulative experience, the good, the ugly, the sublime, the blemished, to infuse his performance.

I want people to bring their own experience to their work.
I don't want empty cups to fill.

Alonzo King, Choreographer.

The view that limitations can be used creatively. Homer Bigart, a famous reporter known for the richness and clarity of his articles, had a pronounced stammer. Rather than feeling stymied by such an impediment, he incorporated the stammer into his persona as a reporter. "G-g-gee. I d-d-didn't really understand that. C-could you repeat it?" He would say to his subject, who would then repeat more slowly and clearly. As a result, Bigart wrote articles with great accuracy and rich quotations.

But every artist labors under limitations. They may be personal—too small, too large hands—financial, societal. Johann Sebastian Bach, while Kantor at Thomas School in Leipzig, had to write a cantata a week, amongst many other duties. This while attentive father to a family that would eventually number twenty. The creative person turns limits into creative fuel. Rather than bemoaning her lot, the artist asks: *how* can I reach my goals given the circumstances I can't change?

The knowledge that she competes only against her own best potential. "A real musician never competes. He plays." Keith Jarrett wrote. Toward that end he uses critical judgment of his performance in the service of understanding and analyzing, not in defeatist criticisms. That means staying *objective while evaluating*. It means asking, "Why doesn't this piece sound better? What should I be changing?" rather than, " This sounds terrible. What's wrong with me?"

Appreciation of the natural world. Nature provides us with connections to our roots, and to the expansiveness, mystery, and duality of the natural world. She soothes and re-invigorates. She provides necessary repose for our souls and time for our music to get integrated. And in our communion with nature, problems are often solved, new insights born. Think of the inventor of Velcro who,

103

while communing with nature yet annoyed by her burrs sticking to his clothing, created an invention that transformed our world.

Think of Nature as a wonderful example of the integrated system. Her world, though unified, is composed of three levels. There is the unseen layer below the ocean's surface, mysterious and primordial; the observable world of man, material and sensual; and the world above, unknowable and spiritual. Communing with nature, then, is a metaphor for communing with our own internal levels: our unconscious, conscious and super-conscious selves. As we've seen in discussing the cross-over moment that performers experience, the act of creating, the act of performing, relies on the fluid connections between all three spheres.

Awareness of one's humorous and playful sides. The creative personality takes life and art seriously, but doesn't take oneself too seriously. Sometimes we get so engrossed in ourselves we lose sight of our relatedness to our art and humanity. Or we miss the wonder and surprise around us.

I once worked with Joseph, whose preoccupation with his piano playing was so intense it was almost painful to witness. He played Brahms for me, musically but with constraint. Without thinking I blurted out, "Hey, man, you play a mean Mozart." He looked up, there was a momentary pause, then—laughter. As he laughed I pointed for him to start playing again. Brahms, humanity restored, breathed more freely. When he'd finished Joseph said, almost sadly, "I didn't know you could joke about classical music." And indeed, why not!

Ira Glass, of National Public Radio, speaking to the graduating journalism class at the University of California, Berkeley, faulted fellow reporters for not finding surprise in their work. "These journalists, I believe, make the world smaller than it is. Theirs is a tiny, crabbed vision of what the world is…The world includes surprises." And without surprise, Glass averred, there is no humor.

Now when you sit down to practice, you are not only a musician but also a creative individual. You are open, wondering, alive and connected. How this facilitates your music-making is the surprise that awaits you.

The following stories show how two adult piano students put methods of integrated practice into use away from the keyboard as well.

Layla, a very talented student, suffered from lupus. Pain often accompanied walking. She very ingeniously devised a way to alleviate pain in her legs by transposing the relaxed arm exercise. Layla took the technique of playing into the keyboard from the released weight of a heavy arm, and practiced taking one step at a time, gently releasing weight into that foot from a relaxed hip joint. She said she imagined the pain dissipating, just as the sound of a note dissipates. And for a while, her pain did dissipate.

Martha, mother, teacher and a most accomplished woman in her own life, never experienced ease with herself. She sat at the edge of the piano bench at her lessons, looking as a younger student might, anxious to please. I asked where else she sat like that. She immediately responded: "At the dinner table. Always ready to jump up if anybody needs anything." After making this connection for herself, Martha was both more relaxed at the keyboard and at dinner, where she enjoyed being with the family in a whole new way, no longer as the sole server, but as the mother who could sometimes be served herself. At practically every subsequent lesson, Martha reported how she became increasingly aware of asserting her rightful place, professionally and personally. Naturally, her new self was reflected in her piano playing as well.

People who practice in this way, have flexibility, fluidity, openness, vitality. It doesn't matter where in your life those qualities are cultivated; they have the power of infusing meaning into all aspects. Let your practicing help you create a life full of beauty, surprise and humor. And let passion and confidence accompany you as you traverse the peaks and valleys of your life.

Notes

THE PREMISES

Roy, Arundhati. *The God of Small Things,* p. 94 New York: Random House, 1997.

CHAPTER 1.

Claudio Arrau, interviewed in "The Art of the Piano, KQED, 1999.
Daniel Siegel, MD. Lecture in Oakland, CA Jan. 12th 2001.

CHAPTER 2.

Wynton Marsalis, History of Jazz, part II. KQED, National
Public Broadcasting.

CHAPTER 3.

Burnshaw, Stanley. *A Seamless Web*, p. 91 New York: George Braziller, 1970.
Levertov, Denise. *The Stream and the Sapphire: Selected Poems on Religious Themes,* p. 6, New York: New Directions, 1997.
USA Weekend, June 25–27, 1999 p.7.
Time Magazine, May 4, 1992.
Record pamphlet accompanying *Fritz Kreisler in Immortal Performances.*

PRACTICE—TITLE PAGE:

Wells, Rebecca. *Little Altars Everywhere*, p 92 HarperPerennial,
A Division of HarperCollins: New York, 1996.

CHAPTER 5.

Star Wars, Episode 1. The Phantom Menace. LucasFilm, 1999.

CHAPTER 7.

Golden, Arthur. *Memoirs of a Geisha,* pp. 152–153. New York:
Alfred A. Knopf, 1997.
Hampshire, Susan. *Susan's Story: Her remarkable life and battle with words,*
Sphere Books Limited, 30–32 Gray's Inn Road, London WC1X 8JL 1983 .

CHAPTER 8.

New York Times, The Living Arts, October 9, 2000, pp. B1–2.
Fang, Siu-wan, *Clara Schumann as Teacher,* D.M.A. Thesis, 1978,
University of Illinois at Urbana-Champaign.

Washington Post article by Bart Barnes reprinted in San Francisco Chronicle, August 7, 2000, pp. 1, A15.

National Public Radio interview with Brenda Blethyn.

Stanislavski, Constantin. *An Actor Prepares*, p.181. New York: Theatre Arts Books, 1984.

Coelho, Paul, *The Illustrated Alchemist,* p 90. New York: HarperCollins, 1993.

PERFORMING—TITLE PAGE

Winokur, Jon, Compiler. *Advice to Writers: A Compendium of Quotes, Anecdotes, & Writerly Wisdom from a Dazzling Array of Literary Lights,* p. 85 New York: Pantheon, 1999.

CODA.

Wolfe, Thomas, *Look Homeward Angel* To the Reader. New York: Simon & Schuster, Inc. Scribner Paperback, 1995.

Cecilia Bartoli, interviewed in San Francisco Focus magazine, December, 1993, p. 86

Wolfe, Thomas, p 4.

Morrison, Toni, *Song of Solomon,* p. 40–41. New York: Plume/Penguin. 1987.

Gehry, New Yorker, p. 41, July 7, 1997.

Ira Glass, Public Radio announcer, speaking to the graduating Journalism Class at Berkeley. North Gate News Vol. 28, Number 6, Spring 2000

Order Form

Please send #_____ copies of

PASSIONATE PRACTICE

The Musician's Guide to Learning, Memorizing and Performing

by Margret Elson

$19.95 per copy
plus shipping and handling: $5 first copy, $1 each additional copy.
(CA residents add $1.65 sales tax per copy)

Total amount enclosed is _____.

_____
Name (please print)

_____
Company

_____
Address

_____
City, State, ZIP

_____
VISA/Mastercard No.   Exp. Date

_____
Signature

_____
Email address

To facilitate your order please send check or money order.

Make checks payable and mail to:
REGENT PRESS
6020-A Adeline, Oakland, CA 94608
phone: 510.547.7602, fax: 510.547.6357
email: regentpress@mindspring.com
or order from our web page: www.regentpress.net